National Trust
Countryside Walks in the

HOME
COUNTIES

Edited by Steve Parker

Photography by John Miller

TRAVELLERS PRESS

Contents

First published in 1985 by
Travellers Press
59 Grosvenor Street,
London W1

ISBN 1 85150 001 4

© Hennerwood Publications
Limited 1985

Printed in Hong Kong

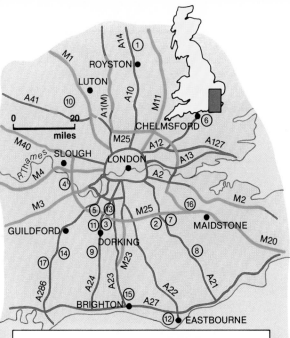

Key to Walk Map Symbols

y/m/a/f	Yards, miles, acres, feet	++++++	Railway
*	Starting point		River or canal
P	Parking/car park		Minor river/stream
i	Information office	====	Waterfall
T	Toilets	)(	Bridge
X	Picnic site		Sea or lake
V	Viewpoint		Sand or beach
⌐	Seat	†††	Woodland
→	Direction of route		Individual tree
⇥	Alternative routes	↓↓↓	Heathland
- - -	Route for walkers		Parkland or green
——	Route for disabled	▲▲▲	Rocks
▬▬	Motorway	○	Cave
——	All other roads		Chalk pit
⟹	One-way traffic	∨∨∨	Marsh or bog
- - -	Ancient way	○	Dew pond
---	Long-distance path	▬	Building
-----	Footpath or track	†	Church or chapel
⟩⟩⟩	Steep descent/ascent	×	Cross
⋯⋯	Steps	∧	Burial mound
▲	Dangerous path	▲	Memorial
∞∞	Wall	△	Youth hostel
⚡	Electric fence	▲	Trigonometric point

Walk Selector

☐ Easy Number	☐ Moderate ☐ Difficult Name	Length (miles)	Time (hours)
1★	**Wimpole Hall & Park**	$2\frac{1}{2}$	$1\frac{1}{2}$
2★	**Toys Hill**	$2\frac{3}{4}$	$1\frac{1}{2}$
3	**Box Hill**	3	2
4★	**Runnymede**	4	2
5	**Bookham Commons**	$5\frac{1}{2}$	3
6★	**Danbury**	$5\frac{1}{2}$	3
7	**Knole Park**	6	3
8	**Scotney Castle**	6	3
9	**Leith Hill**	$6\frac{1}{4}$	3
10	**Ashridge**	$6\frac{3}{4}$	4
11	**Polesden & Ranmore**	$7\frac{1}{2}$	4
12	**Crowlink & Birling**	8	4
13	**Headley & Box Hill**	$8\frac{1}{2}$	$4\frac{1}{2}$
14	**Winkworth**	$8\frac{1}{2}$	$4\frac{1}{2}$
15	**Ditchling Beacon**	$9\frac{3}{4}$	5
16	**Coldrum & Trosley**	11	$5\frac{1}{2}$
17	**Devil's Punch Bowl**	14	7

★ Facilities for disabled people. Fees payable at most car parks (NT parking free for NT members)

Start/finish ℙ Car park	Grid ref	OS map 1:50,000	OS map 1:25,000
Wimpole Hall ℙ	TL 337 510	154/3	TL 25/35
Toys Hill ℙ	TQ 469 517	188	TQ 45/55
Box Hill ℙ	TQ 179 513	187	TQ 05/15
Air Forces Memorial ℙ	SU 996 718	176	SU 87/97 TQ 07/17
Lower Road, Bookham ℙ	TQ 134 545	187	TQ 05/15
Old Armoury ℙ	TL 779 047	167	TL 60/70
Knole House ℙ	TQ 531 547	188	TQ 45/55
Chequers Inn ℙ	TQ 676 362	188	TQ 63/73
Wotton and Abinger Commons ℙ	TQ 131 433	187	TQ 04/14
Bridgewater Monument ℙ	SP 970 131	165	SP 81/91
Polesden Lacey ℙ	TQ 137 525	187	TQ 05/15
Birling Gap ℙ	TV 554 960	199	TV 49/59
Headley Heath ℙ	TQ 205 538	187	TQ 25/35
Winkworth Arboretum ℙ	SU 990 412	186	SU 84/94
Ditchling Beacon ℙ	TQ 332 131	198	TQ 21/31
Trosley Country Park ℙ	TQ 634 612	188	TQ 66/76
Hindhead ℙ	SU 891 358	186	SU 83/93

Introduction

Much of the land covered by the walks in this book belongs to The National Trust for Places of Historic Interest or Natural Beauty. The NT has twin aims: to provide access to its land and buildings where possible, but at the same time to conserve the landscape, its wildlife and its architecture. This means striking a balance between utilization and preservation. Walkers can play their part by following the country code, and of course by supporting the NT.

The rambles have been devised with novice walkers and family outings in mind. But being a novice does not imply being careless or thoughtless. You need to plan your day in advance. First read the walk account and become familiar with the route on good maps. Next, check ahead on opening times and work out a rough schedule of walking, visits, rest and refreshments. Equip yourself with the right kind of clothing

and supplies. Out on the ramble, keep your wits about you: field boundaries may have been moved, trees taken away or new roads constructed.

To give you some idea of what to expect, the walks have been graded. EASY walks take around two hours and are generally well signposted along made-up paths and tracks. MODERATE walks take up to four hours or so; the terrain is mostly firm but there may be an occasional steep climb or rough track. DIFFICULT walks need careful planning, take the best part of a day, and demand detailed maps, compass, refreshments and suitable clothing.

Such detailed planning may seem out of place for a quick trip up Box Hill or a stroll around Wimpole Park, but the moral is: be prepared, enjoy yourself. The Home Counties offer delightful and secluded walking country amongst the bustle of the Outer London sprawl. Toys Hill, just 20 miles from the capital, is one NT property offering tranquillity for the city-dweller. Whatever your interests there is a walk for you – so put one foot in front of the other, and repeat as necessary!

◁ *Fallow deer enjoy the peace of Knole Park near Sevenoaks. The young trees in the park must be protected from their bark-nibbling by stakes and wire cages*

△ *Beautiful but dangerous, a fly agaric from a shady corner of Blakes Wood, Essex*

Countryside Care

The countryside lives and breathes. It is home for many, provides a living for some, and plays a vital role in our economy. It is also the basis of our natural heritage.

Those who walk in the countryside tread a tightrope: between access and conservation, involvement and interference, utilization and preservation. The NT and other organizations are dedicated to preserve our heritage, by ensuring access to certain areas while at the same time planning for the future. Walkers enjoy the highlights of the countryside at their leisure, but they owe it to themselves and others to conserve these pleasures for the generations to come. We have rights, but we also have responsibilities.

RIGHTS OF WAY AND ACCESS
Public footpaths, tracks and bridleways are 'public property' in the same sense as a road or car park. They are not owned by the public; however the landowner, while retaining rights of ownership, 'dedicates' a path or road to public use so that a right of way is established.

A right of way means the public is permitted to cross land by the designated route, without straying from it or causing undue damage. If you leave the path you may be trespassing; if you leave litter, or damage fences or crops, you lay yourself open to legal action. A right of way remains as such until it is revoked ('extinguished') in law, by the local authority. It is irrelevant how often the route is used, or whether it is overgrown, or blocked by a locked gate or a heap of manure. In some cases, however, rights of way may be diverted to permit buildings, roadworks or farming.

Footpaths and other public rights of way are indicated on the Ordnance Survey 1:50,000 (Landranger) series. In addition, public access is customary in common land since fencing it to keep people out is both legally complex and impractical.

Subject to the requirements of farming, forestry, private tenants and the protection of nature, the public is usually given free access to the NT's coast and

FOLLOW THE COUNTRY CODE

The Country Code helps you gain pleasure from the countryside while contributing to its care. Here are some of its main points:

1. Guard against all risk of fire.
2. Fasten all gates.
3. Keep dogs under close control.
4. Keep to public footpaths across farmland.
5. Use gates and stiles to cross fences, hedges and walls.
6. Leave livestock, crops and machinery alone.
7. Take litter home.
8. Help to keep all water clean.
9. Protect wildlife, plants and trees.
10. Take special care on country roads.
11. Make no unnecessary noise.

Above all:

12. Enjoy the countryside and respect its life and work.

country properties at all times. Of course the country code should be observed in these areas as well as elsewhere. Much of the NT's land is farmed, so take extra care to keep on paths in these areas. Details of NT-owned land are given in *Properties of the National Trust* and local publications.

BEWARE OF THE BULL

Complicated bye-laws cover release of bulls into fields crossed by a right of way. It is best to assume that any bull is potentially dangerous and to take a detour or avoid it if possible.

What to Wear

For all but the shortest routes the walker should be properly clothed. Purpose-designed boots and a waterproof top are not only sensible for comfort and safety, they also help you enjoy to the full your day out.

The first essential is some type of water- and windproof outer garment such as an anorak, cagoule or coat, preferably with a hood. Modern lightweight anoraks can be rolled and stowed away when not in use. For warmth the main requirement is several layers of insulating material such as woollen sweaters. These can be taken off as the weather improves, or added to if the wind strengthens. Wool 'breathes' to minimize sweating yet retains body heat effectively. A thick, warm shirt is also recommended.

Denim jeans are a bad choice for legwear. They are usually too restrictive and have poor insulating qualities. Walking trousers should be warm and comfortably loose to allow movement without chafing. On long walks carry waterproof overtrousers.

Feet are the walker's best friends, so care for them. Strong leather walking boots with studded or non-slip soles are the ideal choice. Good ankle support is a must in rocky and difficult terrain. For short walks on easy ground a pair of tough, comfortable shoes may be adequate. Wellingtons may be suited to very wet ground but quickly become uncomfortable and tend to rub up blisters. Whatever the footwear, thick woollen socks (two pairs, if possible) are the sensible choice beneath. Footwear *must be broken in* and fit comfortably before you take to the paths.

On longer walks it is wise to carry a few extras in your rucksack: a sweater, a spare pair of socks, a warm hat and a pair of woollen gloves.

▷ *The well-dressed walker pauses to consult the map. Many people new to rambling are surprised at how chilled they become after a couple of hours in the open air, away from warm rooms or the car heater. Even on sunny days the wind and a few hundred feet of altitude can make you feel uncomfortably cool. The moral: Be prepared!*

◁ *The wisdom of being well prepared pays off when you get halfway round the walk and the rain closes in*

Woollen sweater

Waterproof anorak

Comfortable legwear

Walking boots

11

What to Take

Certain items are basic to any respectable walk. A rucksack and good maps are vital. Other equipment depends on the nature of the walk and personal interests.

The rucksack or backpack has many advantages over a hand-carried bag. With a rucksack you can take more, carry it more comfortably, and leave your hands free (an important safety consideration in rough terrain). There is an enormous variety of rucksacks available. For a half-day or day walk choose a medium-sized model of about 20 litres capacity, made of nylon or similar, that fits you snugly without chafing.

A selection of maps should always be at hand. Do not rely solely on the sketch maps in this book. These sketch maps are intended for use with Ordnance Survey maps (1:50,000 *Landranger* series or, better, the *Outdoor Leisure Maps* and others at 1:25,000, about $2\frac{1}{2}$

▷ *A hot drink brings a welcome feeling of inner comfort on a long walk, while glucose or chocolate bars provide ready energy*
▽ *Don't forget the nature-lover's second pair of eyes*

inches to the mile). A good map provides details of rights of way, viewpoints, parking, conveniences and telephones, and lets you identify distant features (see page 14). A compass is necessary for map-reading since paths are often indistinct or routes unmarked across open country. Local guidebooks and field guides point out items of interest as you go, rather than after you return.

On a long walk carry nourishment with you unless you are sure of a 'refuelling' stop. Concentrated high-energy food such as chocolate or mintcake revives flagging limbs and spirits, and a modern lightweight vacuum-flask provides a welcome hot beverage. A few sticking plasters, a penknife and a length of string may come in handy so keep them in a side pocket in your rucksack.

Walking is an excellent way of reaching an unusual viewpoint or approaching wary wildlife. A camera records the scene and 'collects' nature without damaging it, and binoculars permit close-ups of animals about their business. Walk with these items at the ready – you never know when they might be needed.

A compass is essential; a 35mm camera outfit is less so, though a pocket version may come in useful

Maps

A walker without a map is like a car without a steering wheel. It is essential to obtain good maps, learn how to read and interpret them, and check your route before you set off. Most experienced walkers use a combination of maps, as described below. The sketch maps in this book are not intended to be your sole guide: use them in combination with Ordnance Survey (OS) and other maps in guide books and local publications.

The OS maps come in two main scales. First is the *Landranger* 1:50,000 series (about $1\frac{1}{4}$ inches to the mile). These maps cover the entire country and show footpaths, bridleways, rights of way, farm buildings and other features. They are useful for general planning and for gaining an overall impression of the area.

The second main OS scale is 1:25,000 (roughly $2\frac{1}{2}$ inches to the mile). These maps are published as individual sheets of the *First* and *Second Series* covering the entire country, and as large fold-out *Outdoor Leisure Maps* for recreational areas, holiday regions and national parks. The 1:25,000 maps are often called the 'walker's maps' since they show features important to walkers and ramblers, such as field boundaries,

▽ *In the National Grid referencing system the first three numbers are the* Easting *(left to right), the second three numbers are the* Northing *(bottom to top), and the reference is accurate to within 100 metres (110 yards)*

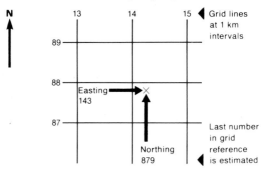

viewpoints, rescue posts and rights of way. Up-to-date 1:25,000 maps are recommended for use with the maps in this book. Further information is available from the Ordnance Survey (see address on page 127).

Another useful series is the *Footpath Maps* published by the Ramblers' Association (RA). These are at 1:25,000 scale and show many details such as footpaths, tracks, rides and bridleways, car parks and gates. For details of regions covered by these maps contact a local RA representative via a regional newspaper or community magazine, or enquire at the RA Head Office (for address see page 127).

Safety

Most of the routes described in this book can be completed safely by the average family, provided basic safety rules are observed. In more remote country, such as the Lake District, extra precautions are required.

1 Wear suitable clothing and footwear, as described in the previous pages.

2 Always assume the weather may suddenly turn nasty. Carry an extra sweater and an anorak, or cagoule, or even a small umbrella.

3 Obtain a good map and learn to read it. The maps in this book are intended for use in conjunction with detailed walkers' maps such as the Ordnance Survey 1:25,000 series.

4 On longer walks take some energy-giving food such as chocolate or glucose lozenges and a drink of some kind.

5 Allow plenty of time to complete your walk. A good average is two miles per hour, less if you enjoy views or watch nature at work.

6 If possible, have a first-aider in the group, and take change for emergency phone calls.

Wimpole Hall & Park

Wimpole Hall with its landscaped gardens and beautiful park, and the Wimpole Home Farm with its rare breeds of livestock, provide a complete day out in the countryside south-west of Cambridge. This walk tours the gardens and park, parts of which are expertly landscaped with exotic trees while others are pleasantly natural and overgrown.

The Wimpole Estate, over 2,400a, is the setting for this $2\frac{1}{2}$m perimeter ramble through undulating parkland, wood and landscaped garden. A 1m detour on the walk takes you to visit the folly near the lake in the centre of the park. The walk is particularly suitable for families, with the lake, picnic area and adventure playground, plus a children's area in the restored Home Farm for rare breeds of livestock. The Hall itself provides refreshments and there are walled gardens, while the park is the result of the endeavours of the three great landscape designers, Charles Bridgeman, Capability Brown and Humphrey Repton. For those

△ *Wimpole Hall, bequeathed in 1976 by Mrs Bambridge*

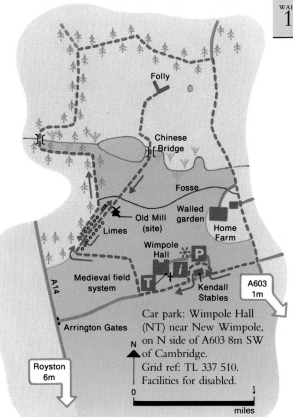

Folly

Chinese
Bridge

Fosse

Old Mill
(site)

Walled
garden

Limes

Home
Farm

Wimpole
Hall

P

* **i**

Medieval field
system

T

+

Kendall
Stables

A603
1m

A14

Arrington Gates

Car park: Wimpole Hall
(NT) near New Wimpole,
on N side of A603 8m SW
of Cambridge.
Grid ref: TL 337 510.
Facilities for disabled.

N

Royston
6m

0   ¼

miles

who enjoy peace and quiet there are tranquil areas in
the park, with fine views over Cambridgeshire.
Several booklets and leaflets describing the house,
gardens, farm and walk in great detail are available
from the NT shop and kiosk near the car park.

If you drive to Wimpole Hall along the A14, the old
Roman road of Ermine Way, note the replanted
avenue of limes to the right. These trees, well protected
in strong wire casings against deer and rabbits, were
grafted from large specimens on the Wimpole Estate.

As you leave the car park there is a small chapel and
statuesque trees, including a magnificent turkey oak

17

△ *Looking north across the Chinese Bridge to the Gothic folly*

planted in 1910. Follow the gravel path that skirts a wide lawn to the south of the house. Wimpole Hall was begun in 1640 by Sir Thomas Cicheley and is the largest country house in Cambridgeshire. Looking towards the great house there is an enormous lime tree, in season heavy with blossom and bees. To the west of the house is a planted arboretum, with trees of many different shapes and lush foliages.

Keep the iron paddock railings to your left and walk on to notice, usually occupying the paddock, a herd of white cattle. They are British White, an extremely attractive breed with black ears and muzzles. They are one of the many examples of livestock maintained by the adjacent Home Farm, managed by the NT.

A few hundred yards after passing the south facade of the house there is a stile into a field. Keep to the right, with woodland on your right, and walk up a grassy slope. Some 150y along you can see to the left the pronounced ridges and furrows of the medieval field system and an elegant avenue of walnut trees. Higher still on your left is a field usually populated by longhorn cattle.

The path now changes direction north–east over a stile and through a grand avenue of limes dating back to 1795. At the end of the avenue to the right is a clump of more lime trees surrounding an ice house, once the site of a windmill. At the end of the avenue is a good view of undulating fields and parkland, with the lake straight ahead tucked into a tree-bordered hollow and the Gothic tower folly in the distance.

The path leads down to a broad ditch or fosse with simple steps set into the bank, then up to another stile. Once through this field you approach the lake through a kissing gate to the Chinese Bridge. This graceful structure has been completely rebuilt, including the raised wooden slats to prevent horses from slipping on the smooth wooden surface. The lake itself is fringed with reeds at its northern edge, and in summer yellow waterlilies flower and coot and moorhen scuttle about. Once you cross the bridge, the folly looms large beyond a field of corn. Walk around the field with hedgerows and thickets to the left. There is nothing behind the folly's facade, although the central tower will hopefully be restored to allow visitors to view the countryside from four storeys high.

After examining the folly, walk leisurely back to rejoin the start of the longer perimeter walk towards the end of the avenue of limes, on the right (north-west). It starts by running north-east, parallel to the avenue, then branches north.

This perimeter walk is along well-marked tracks through woodland, clockwise around the estate. The track is rough and may be muddy in places. In summer the wild privet bushes are in flower and dog's mercury carpets the floor. There are views of farmland to the west, and farther on the path is flanked by tall, spindly ash trees with only crowns of foliage. The path dog-legs over a bridge that crosses the lake's stream outlet. At the north-western edge of the estate the track diverges; take the right-hand branch out of the woods to the edge of the cornfield. The folly stands to the south.

Continue along the northern edge of the park, then turn right into the road (A603) and follow it south back towards the Hall. You can visit the rare livestock breeds in Home Farm, wander around the great house, examine the walled garden or simply relax and admire the beautiful surroundings.

▷ *Lime's sweet blossoms have a honeysuckle-like smell that is irresistible to bees; they ripen into small downy fruits*

Toys Hill

Toys Hill, south-west of Sevenoaks in Kent, is a place of beauty and peace — yet only 20m from central London. The sandstone summit is capped by woods but there are several fine viewpoints and a wealth of wildlife in the ancient beech and oak groves.

The woods on the sandstone of Toys Hill, nearly 800f high, are varied and unusual, with fantastic ancient pollarded beeches. The 2¾m route leads from the hilltop car park down into a valley to the east, and back over the hill to the west side; so there are some quite steep slopes, and a couple of long flights of steps. The

△ *Bough Beech reservoir to the south-west of Toys Hill*

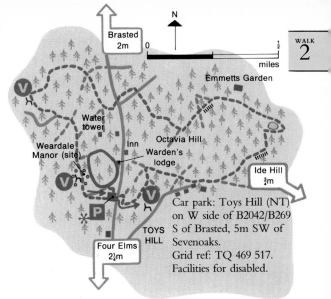

Brasted
2m

N

0   ½
                                      miles

Emmetts Garden

Water
tower

Weardale
Manor (site)

Inn

Octavia Hill
Warden's
lodge

Ide Hill
¾m

TOYS
HILL

Four Elms
2½m

Car park: Toys Hill (NT)
on W side of B2042/B269
S of Brasted, 5m SW of
Sevenoaks.
Grid ref: TQ 469 517.
Facilities for disabled.

path is clearly waymarked, and firm underfoot. The
entire walk is on NT land, and there are local maps and
leaflets describing Toys Hill available from the Warden's Lodge 250y north of the car park.

From the car park, cross the road and follow the
path into the Octavia Hill Woodlands (named after
one of the NT's founders, who lived nearby).
Throughout the walk, follow the red waymarks
painted on posts. The path winds down through
beechwoods, where little but holly and a variety of
autumn toadstools such as *Boletus* and *Russula* can
grow under the dense canopy. Soon you reach a
viewpoint with seats, and magnificent views eastwards
to the church spire on Ide Hill (another NT property)
and south-west over the Bough Beech Reservoir to
the distant hills of Ashdown Forest.

Keep right at the next crossing. The weirdly-shaped
beeches used to be 'pollarded' – that is, their branches
were cut off at head height every 15 years or so, giving
a crop of poles for firewood, charcoal and building.
The tree would resprout, safely out of reach of
browsing animals. Until 1853 Toys Hill was
commonland – part of the common of Brasted Chart –
and the people of Brasted had rights to graze cattle and
pigs, gather firewood and quarry churtstone.

The path falls gradually for about ½m. Keep left near the bottom of the wood and ignore the path over the stile ahead that leads to Ide Hill. The woods are different here, with a thick undergrowth of bramble, bracken and bluebells under oak and hazel. At the foot of a flight of steps you emerge into the light of the coppiced alder woods of Pugden, with a riot of summer flowers and warblers singing in the thickets. 'Coppiced' trees are cut regularly at ground level so that several slender trunks grow from one root system. Toys Hill is rated of national importance for nature conservation as a grade 1 site of special scientific interest, because of the clear sequence of plant communities from the dry, acid hilltop beechwoods, through lower woods of oak, birch and hazel, to the wet alkaline alder fen of Pugden.

Turn right to skirt the spring-fed pond that used to supply water to Emmetts House on the hillside above (another NT property, with gardens open to the public). As you climb up past the pond, there is a grassy meadow above which offers a fine view and a break from the shady woods. The path climbs gently out of Pugden, with hazel coppice gradually giving way to oak, then beech and holly again. Keep left up a flight of steps, duck under a barrier, and cross the bridlepath. The bilberry growing extensively in these woods has black berries that make excellent pies and jam.

The slope flattens as you reach the hilltop, and the path merges with the green waymarks. Keep to the

△ *Walking eastwards through Octavia Hill woodlands*

△ *Western hemlock, a shade-tolerant and fast-growing conifer planted for timber*
▷ *Alder prefers watersides and lowland fen*

right. The hilltop is scarred with pits where chert and gravel have been quarried over the centuries for building and roadstone – most recently by Acorn Camp volunteers for surfacing the paths. Cross the road, keep left, and shortly cross the road again. The beech and oak here were coppiced in the last century.

Keep right along the red waymarked route, which falls gradually through heathy woods with thickets of shallon and rhododendron. Near the foot of the hill are dark young plantations of Scots pine and western hemlock (*Tsuga heterophylla*), as well as impressive mature pines. Before climbing the hill again there is a good view across the clay vale to the North Downs. The coppiced beeches you can see on the slope above are being 'stored', with one or two stems of each tree being left to grow into big timber.

The path turns left on to the former rear drive of Weardale Manor, and banks of rhododendron and shallon indicate a garden ahead. In fact, Weardale Manor has gone; the grand house was built in 1906 by Lord Weardale, of the Stanhope family, and demolished by 1940. A clump of pines marks where the house stood on its terrace, but all around the woods have reinvaded. Leave Weardale by the ruined entrance gates and keep right, down the slope, to the chert pits hiding the car park.

Box Hill

Box Hill is one of the most famous viewpoints in the south of England. This figure-8 walk takes in the edge of the chalk-faced escarpment with its unique flora and fauna, the wooded summit and the exhilarating views along the North Downs and across to the South Downs.

Box Hill is justly famous for the views from its chalk-faced scarp that looks south and west. On a clear day the scene extends to Crowborough Beacon about 25m away. The 3m walk is a gentle figure-8 with one loop along the ridge of the chalk scarp face, the other loop through the shady beech, birch and yew groves to the north and west of the viewpoint. Box Hill is a grade 1 site of special scientific interest and a designated area of outstanding natural beauty; because of its proximity to London it receives thousands of visitors daily in summer so please be particularly careful.

▽ *The views from Box Hill over Surrey and Sussex*

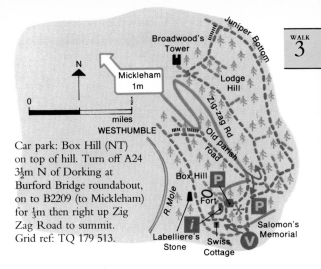

Broadwood's
Tower

N

Mickleham
1m

0 ──────── ½
miles

WESTHUMBLE

Juniper Bottom

Lodge
Hill

Zig-zag Rd

Old parish road

Box Hill P

R.Mole

Fort

P

Labelliere's
Stone

Swiss
Cottage

Salomon's
Memorial

V

Car park: Box Hill (NT)
on top of hill. Turn off A24
3½m N of Dorking at
Burford Bridge roundabout,
on to B2209 (to Mickleham)
for ⅓m then right up Zig
Zag Road to summit.
Grid ref: TQ 179 513.

From the NT car park cross the road towards the
kiosk and turn left to visit the NT shop and
Information Centre. Continue on the path to about
50y past the shop until you reach a wide gravel drive to
the right, with an old gnarled tree trunk in the centre.
Follow this track, and gates to the private grounds of
the NT-owned Swiss Cottage are on your left. The

△ *From The Whites on Box Hill there are marvellous views across the River Mole and Dorking Gap to Ranmore*

cottage was built in the early nineteenth century and James Logie Baird experimented there with early television transmission.

Ignore the track that goes right to the rear of the NT shop; instead climb over the log and follow the track through brambles and rosebay willowherb into thickening birch and beech woodland. Pass a large yew and adjacent turkey oak on the left. You now join the NT waymarked walk coming from the left. The steep slope down to the left is crossed by the North Downs Way long-distance path which descends steeply to the River Mole in the valley. The old woods which cling to the steepest slopes are almost entirely yew and box, since these are the only trees with root systems deep and strong enough.

The box trees that give their name to the hill appear repeatedly in the long history of the area. The rent for cutting box wood was first recorded in 1608, at £50 per year. Box has long been prized for its hard, close, golden grain and it was used for musical instruments, inlays and fine carvings.

The path bears right and passes Major Peter Labelliere's Stone. The eccentric Dorking marine was originally buried upside-down so that he would be the right way up at the end of this 'topsy-turvy' world.

Follow the red arrows (marking the Box Hill Short Walk) north out on to the open, grassy slope known as The Whites, where you can pause to relish the views. To the north-west are Leatherhead and Ashtead; west (left) is the hamlet of Westhumble; and down below is the luxury of the Burford Bridge Hotel. Staine

Street, a Roman road from Chichester to London, forded the River Mole near where the hotel is now, on its way through the gap in the North Downs. The slopes to the right of The Whites were cleared in neolithic times; the NT permits sheep to graze there in winter, otherwise trees would eventually cover the area and the unique grassland plants and animals would disappear. Among the grasses you may find small scabious, milkwort, violet, marjoram and the delicate harebell. Grasshoppers, butterflies and other small creatures busy themselves in the flowers. Where the white chalk is exposed, it is dry on wet days – and damp on dry days. This is due to chalk's porous nature, which keeps these slopes green and lush whatever the weather.

Continue straight along the wide, worn, grassy path past a red arrow; about 50y farther is another red arrow to the right of the path, pointing at right-angles to some wooden steps down the slope to the right. Descend and cross the flint-and-grass track that runs along a wire fence, where the wayfaring trees bear their bright red berries in August. Continue down the next flight of 118 wooden steps towards the Zig Zag Valley, turning right just before you reach the road. Follow the road south-east for 50y until the old parish path leads off to the right. Follow this well-trodden path up the valley and into the wood where a massive yew tree has been trimmed to allow passage. Some of the yews hereabouts may be up to 1,000 years old.

△ *Sheep-grazing in Zig Zag Valley preserves the habitat*

The less-steep slopes in this wood are thickly cloaked with yew, box, ash, beech and oak. Patches of dog's mercury and other shade-tolerant flowers grow where light penetrates. There is much old, dead wood on these ancient slopes and the chalk-induced damp conditions are ideal for bracket, coral and other fungi and many mosses and ferns.

Continue up the fairly steep flint gully, cross straight over the Zig Zag Road with care at its sharp bend, and proceed upwards past bramble and wild raspberry. About 20y past the road the path splits at three huge beech trees. If you have had enough, follow the red arrow right, back to the car park.

Those who are still eager should take the left fork at the three beeches, through the trees to join a well-worn track coming from the right. Turn left on to this and you are now following the grey arrows of the NT Nature Trail. This path is also a horse ride, so beware if you have small children or dogs. The wide track, muddy in places even in a dry summer, passes north-west through the old mixed woodland of Lodge Hill. Beech is the dominant species on this chalk plateau; many have lived out their 150-year lives and are gradually being replaced. Note the young trees to the left of the track; the beech plantings are interspersed with larch and Corsican pine to provide initial protection. The pines are removed before they become a threat to the beech. Grey squirrels abound, to the detriment of the trees – they may eventually

△ *Downland meadow on the approach to Broadwood's Folly*

decimate the beeches here. Roe deer are also a problem since they graze on tree shoots.

The path carries straight on, marked by grey arrows, until the downland meadow opens out ahead. The view is across the Zig Zag Valley (the first half of the walk) to the village of Westhumble and the continuation of the North Downs Ridge. Ranmore Common (walk 11) is beyond. In summer the myriad wildflowers indicate the chalky soil type beneath: wild marjoram, field gentian, St John's-wort, sainfoin and purple milk vetch. If you sit quietly on a sunny afternoon the wildlife comes to you: grass-hoppers by the dozen, ladybirds, and 40 of the 66 British species of butterfly – including blues, skippers, coppers, meadow brown, speckled wood and brim-stone – have been seen here.

Back on the path, enter the wood ahead and you are confronted by the tower of Broadwood's Folly. This was built by the piano manufacturer Thomas Broadwood when he purchased the nearby Juniper Hall (now a Field Study Centre) in 1814. It may have been a signal tower but is now dwarfed by surround-ing beech trees. Follow the grey arrows to the right, through the less-dense woodland of sycamore, hazel, pine and ash and the correspondingly dense under-growth of nettle, bramble, thistle and bracken. Bear left at the fork and follow the path, right at the next fork and down the hill. The larger trees here were destroyed and there is dense growth of young ones.

△ *The quiet, secluded path along Lodge Hill ridge*

▽ *As you would expect, box flourishes on Box Hill. Its flowers are petal-less, consisting only of four stamens (male) or three styles (female flower)*

As the hill gets steeper you emerge over Juniper Bottom, or Happy Valley. This grass plain is grazed only by rabbits and since the days of myxomatosis it has been encroached by shrubs such as wayfaring tree, dogwood and elder. The 103 steps take you to the bottom, where you turn right along the flint track which ascends back to a steepish, dense and dark wood of box and yew. Turn right at the next junction and proceed straight on at the following junction, through the trees to emerge on Donkey Green.

Box Hill has long been a venue for sightseeing. When the railway arrived in 1867, day-trippers from London swarmed over the hill and children enjoyed donkey rides on this green. Cross the grass and over the road to the visual climax of the walk – the 563f viewpoint at the site of Salomon's Memorial. This structure was erected in honour of Leopold Salomon after he gave Box Hill to the NT in 1914. To the right and below is the River Mole, with Dorking just beyond. Above the town is Leith Hill, the highest point in SE England at 965f. At the bottom of Box Hill the line of the iron-age Pilgrim's Way is visible running approximately with the electricity pylons. Far away to the left the South Downs are often visible, 25m away. To the south-east you may see aircraft flying low as they approach or leave Gatwick Airport. The semicircular stone indicator provides details of the landscape to supplement your maps. After enjoying the view return to the road and follow it to the left, back to the NT shop and refreshments.

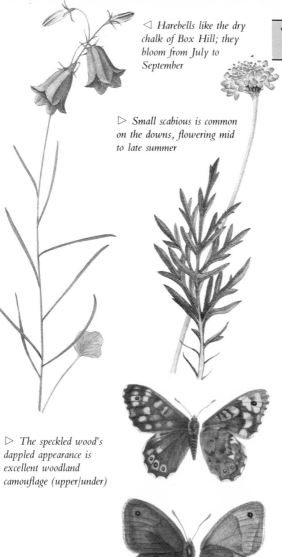

◁ *Harebells like the dry chalk of Box Hill; they bloom from July to September*

▷ *Small scabious is common on the downs, flowering mid to late summer*

▷ *The speckled wood's dappled appearance is excellent woodland camouflage (upper/under)*

▷ *The meadow brown is a lazy insect, preferring to hide among leaves (upper/under)*

31

Runnymede

This walk embraces the adjacent NT sites of Runnymede Meadows and Cooper's Hill Slopes, on the south bank of the Thames between Windsor and Staines. There are three famous memorials on the route, a stroll along the towpath, and commanding views from the top of Cooper's Hill.

This 4m walk takes in open meadows, riverbank and the partly wooded slopes of Cooper's Hill to give an interesting variety of scenery and habitat. The route embraces virtually the whole of the NT's Runnymede Meadows (188a) and Cooper's Hill Slopes (110a) and visits three famous but very different monuments: the Air Forces Memorial to airmen of the Second World War; the John F Kennedy Memorial in honour of the great American president; and the Magna Carta Memorial on the historic meads, near the banks of stately 'Old Father Thames'. The paths up and down Cooper's Hill are steep in places and sections may be muddy after rain. .

Return to the entrance of the Air Forces Memorial car park. Turn left along Cooper's Hill Lane and follow the red brick wall of Brunel University's

△ *Looking down to the meads from Oak Lane, near the start*

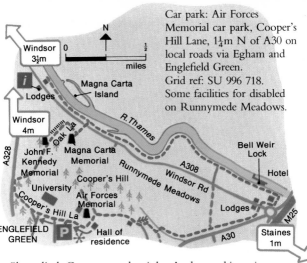

Car park: Air Forces Memorial car park, Cooper's Hill Lane, $1\frac{1}{4}$m N of A30 on local roads via Egham and Englefield Green.
Grid ref: SU 996 718.
Some facilities for disabled on Runnymede Meadows.

Shoreditch Campus on the right. At the road junction ahead, at the top of Priest Hill (A328), turn right and walk downhill on the roadside verge for about 200y, then turn right into the tree-lined tarmac track of Oak Lane. After the tennis courts on the right, enter woodland ahead, and descend to reach the John F Kennedy Memorial. This large block of Portland stone, erected in 1965, stands in an acre of ground given by Britain to the people of America, in memory of their great president who was assassinated on 22 November 1963 in Dallas, Texas.

△ *Walking along Oak Lane, approaching the memorials*

33

Continue on the cobblestone steps, down the hill to emerge from trees by a wooden swing gate on to the historic and unspoilt Runnymede Meadows. These were given to the NT in 1931 by Lady Fairhaven and her two sons, in memory of her husband. The benefactors also provided the two pairs of small roadside lodges, designed by Sir Edwin Lutyens, which mark the eastern and western extents of the meadows. The two lodges away to the left, at the Windsor end, serve as the Magna Carta Information Room and Tea Rooms respectively.

Turn right along the edge of the meadows for nearly 200y to the Magna Carta Memorial – a temple-like structure erected in 1957 by the members of the American Bar Association. The event commemorated is of course the granting of the Magna Carta by King John in these meadows on 15 June 1215.

Now turn left across the meadows, following the fence on your right. Cross the A308 main road with great care and the River Thames is ahead, with Magna Carta Island opposite. The Lutyens lodges referred to above are to be seen to the left about 300y along the road. Turn right to follow the bank downstream along a gravel track. After about 200y keep to the right of a tree-lined backwater and continue along the riverside

△ *The rich Thames-side meadows make good grazing land*

△ *Memorial to Magna Carta, cornerstone of British democracy*

for almost 1½m downstream to Bell Weir Lock. This stretch of the Thames is busy during summer with craft of all shapes and sizes; the peace of the evening may be disturbed by a hired 'bar-and-disco' cruiser on its way back to Windsor or Staines. In the quieter months the occasional angler props up a camping chair while a good variety of waterbirds, including heron, ripple the river's surface.

Continue on the towpath past Bell Weir lock to just before the road bridges ahead – the far one has recently been constructed for the M25 motorway. Turn right on a gravel track to reach the main A30; here turn right along a footway, past the Runnymede Hotel on the right, to reach the memorials and the other pair of Lutyens lodges marking the eastern end of Runny-mede Meadows. With care, turn left to re-cross the A308 and continue across the grass, soon to follow the southern edge of meadows with the Egham bypass (A30) running nearby on the left.

Cross over the end of a tarmac path that heads into the meads and after about 300y bear right away from the bypass, with a hedge and then a fence on your left. You arrive at a stile next to a gate, just after crossing a shallow ditch. Over the stile, turn right along the edge of a field for about 130y to another stile on the right;

here turn left, steeply uphill through the middle of a field to a further stile. Now turn right, along the sunken gravel track that climbs past the property of Grand View on the left. Eventually you emerge from the woodland at the top of Cooper's Hill, with the meadows and the Thames glistening below.

Follow the road through left- and right-hand bends with Kingswood, a students' residence for Royal Holloway College, on the left. On your right are the trimmed holly hedges of the Air Forces Memorial. Built and maintained by the Commonwealth War Graves Commission, this beautiful and peaceful cloistered white stone building was unveiled in 1953 and records the names of 20,000 airmen who died during the Second World War and who have no known grave. From the top of the building's tower there are fine views over the countryside to the north, with glimpses through the tall trees of Windsor, the River Thames, Runnymede Meadows and the buildings of London's Heathrow Airport. To complete the walk, continue along Cooper's Hill Road for a further 250y to return to the car park at the start.

△ *The Thames' graceful sweep near Magna Carta Island*

△ Herons fish in the quieter
stretches of the Thames near
Runnymede and can often be
seen flying past

△ Weeping willow's catkins
appear in April, with the
leaves; its slender hanging
branches adorn Thames banks ▷

37

Bookham Commons

In contrast to the high chalk country of Box
Hill to the south, this walk reveals a detailed
wealth of clay-based lowland wildlife on the
richly-wooded Bookham Commons just west
of Leatherhead. Trees and bird inhabitants are
particularly varied and present the nature-lover
with an absorbing day out.

Bookham and Banks Commons together form a 447a
NT property which has been kept under study by
members of the London Natural History Society for
more than 40 years. Consequently an enormous
amount is known about the natural history of the
commons. This 5½m walk provides no high
viewpoints; its fascination lies in watching nature at
close quarters, going about its daily business.
Bookham village clings to its attractive appearance
despite the 'infill' developments rife in this area of
Outer London. Parts of the walk are muddy in wet
weather, so come prepared.

From the car park entrance turn right on to Lower
Road, towards the church. Cross carefully to the gate
of the churchyard. There has been a place of worship at
the site of St Nicholas Church since the original Saxon

△ *St Nicholas Church, Bookham, at the walk's start*

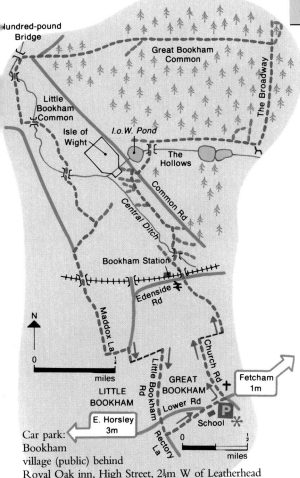

Car park:
Bookham
village (public) behind
Royal Oak inn, High Street, 2½m W of Leatherhead
on A246 (to Guildford). Turn N into High Street,
W at church, car park on left. Grid ref: TQ 134 545.

settlement of the fifth century. Proceed along Church
Road, northwards, following the ancient Roman way
of Staine Street from Chichester to London. The
Tyrells on the left-hand side of the road, now a doctors'
surgery, is seventeenth-century; farther along on the

39

△ *A grassy clearing on the way to Isle of Wight Pond*

right are Church Cottages, built in the fifteenth and sixteenth centuries on the site of a slaughter yard.

Continue past various shops, then houses and driveways, until the NT Commons open out in a wide green triangle. Follow the path that forks left along the left-hand side of the common. Go across Edenside Road and on to Bookham BR station. Cross the road to the station car park. The building behind you was once the Merrylands Temperance Hotel, built by Mrs Chrystie who, with her sister-in-law, worked hard at the turn of the century to rid Bookham of alcohol by buying up many of the ale houses.

Cross the railway line (opened in 1885) by the footbridge on the right and go through the kissing gate on to NT land again. Bear right over a plank bridge crossing the Central Ditch and follow a worn grassy path left through the thickening scrub of bramble, oak, and crab apple trees on the right.

Cross a clearing, usually thick with bracken in summer, and turn left on to a sandier path that weaves its way north through recently cleared areas that bore birch saplings. All along the walk is evidence of the way the commons are managed to maintain a patchwork of habitats, from open grass to scrub to young wood and the fine old mature oaks.

Bear left as a path runs in from the right. In August and September the red berries of bryony brighten the greenery, while at any time of year the robins can be heard arguing in the holly and hawthorn. Pass clumps of birch and bracken in a grassy clearing, and new willows planted near a fork in the path. Take the right fork and pass willowherb and honeysuckle; go right at the next crossroads; and straight on at the next. The grassy track leads past the fenced-off Isle of Wight area on the left. Where a path joins on the left, go right and cross the wide Common Road that runs north-west.

Ahead is the Isle of Wight Pond, which was silting up and turning into marsh before it was renovated in 1972/3. Moorhen, coot and mallard swim on the surface while frogs, toads and newts breed underneath. Follow the path along the south-east side of the pond to the wooden bridge over the stream running in from a pond on the right. In summer notice the watermint, marigold and rushes. Cross the bridge and turn right on to the wide bridlepath which runs eastwards along an area known as The Hollows.

The commons lie on London clay 400f thick in places and here in The Hollows the ground is waterlogged for most of the year. Pass two more ponds on the right, edged by reeds and rushes with hazel, yew, sycamore and oak trees. In spring the oak tortrix moth caterpillars dangle on their fine threads from the branches, forming a giant web across the path.

Cross a plank bridge and go straight over the next junction where bulrushes thrive to the right. The path rises gently and continues ahead where the bridleway, marked with a blue arrow, branches to the left. At the park bench under a spreading oak turn left under the

△ *Fisherman (with licence!) enjoys Isle of Wight Pond*

anti-horse bar on to a wide grassy track named the Broadway. Wildflowers such as scabious, tormentil and white clover grow in the grass and in autumn there are fungi along the damp edges of this cutting.

Past another anti-horse bar and 150y farther three paths form a triangle around a clump of trees and bushes. Take the left-hand sandy path. This long and fairly straight horse track is wide and muddy in its dips. Follow the blue arrows, straight on at a crossroads with bars to the left and right, and go right at the next fork. Walk on past a path that joins from the left, and ignore a track that leaves to the left. Straight on you arrive at a crossing clearing where, below the ground, large drainage pipes serve Bookham householders.

Go across the clearing and back into the trees, past a fenced field with buildings on the right. The path descends to Hundred-Pound Bridge car park. The original road that crossed the Bookham stream was constructed by Saxons when Bookham belonged to Chertsey Abbey. Do not cross the bridge, but turn left under the bar and along the small path running along the left bank of the stream. You are now walking into more open country, grazed for over 1,000 years until local residents clubbed together, bought the commons and presented them to the NT for safe keeping. Clay is still near the surface and the many varieties of rushes indicate the dampness underfoot.

Cross a plank bridge and proceed past vetches, hops and thistles. This low scrub is rich in bird life, particularly finches such as greenfinch, hawfinch, bullfinch and of course busy bands of chaffinch. You arrive at a large path junction; turn left immediately before reaching the gravel road. There is a sign announcing *Bookham Commons* and one prohibiting horse-riding except on the designated horse tracks. Follow the wide horse track over a concrete bridge and then straight on, ignoring the left turn. Shortly there is another anti-horse bar on the right and you go under it, beneath an oak, and through an oak-and-hawthorn thicket. The path winds on to a junction. Follow the way that leads over a wooden-sided bridge and eventually you come into line with overhead tele-phone wires, and the Bookham Grange Hotel appears ahead. Follow the path to the right and turn left on to the metalled road. Refreshments are available at the

△ *Heading east from Rectory Lane back to the village*

hotel and the road in front of it leads east, round a corner and over a bridge where a left turn takes you back to Bookham station.

A more attractive return route is to walk along the stony lane to the right (west) of the hotel, over the railway, and on to metalled Maddox Lane that bends left to Little Bookham Street. Turn right and walk back to the village. The NT owns the grass verges as far as The Windsor Castle pub, which is a listed building like many in the lane.

At the top of Little Bookham Street cross Lower Road with care to the left-hand side of Rectory Lane. Walk ahead and there is a path to the left opposite the Preston Cross Country Club. Follow this path to the playing fields and continue along the line of trees to the far corner. Emerge on to the Lower Road again, turn right and the car park is a few hundred yards along past the Baptist Hall, school and other village buildings.

◁ *Common frogs abound on the wet clays of Bookham, breeding in the many ponds and ditches*

▷ *The common toad is heavier, darker and wartier than its fellow amphibian, the frog; also it walks rather than hops*

Danbury

The undulating, well-wooded country east of Chelmsford is the setting for this lovely walk through the parishes of Danbury and Little Baddow. The route takes in almost every type and stage of woodland development, also low-lying boggy areas and agricultural land.

This varied and interesting 5½m walk winds through many different habitats as it links three main NT sites (and passes several minor ones): Danbury Common and Lingwood Common, 300f above sea level and 214¼a total; and in the parish of Little Baddow the 105½a of Blake's Wood. Part of Danbury Common, called the Backwarden, is let to the Essex Naturalists' Trust as a nature reserve, and Blake's Wood is also managed as a reserve by this trust. You should take

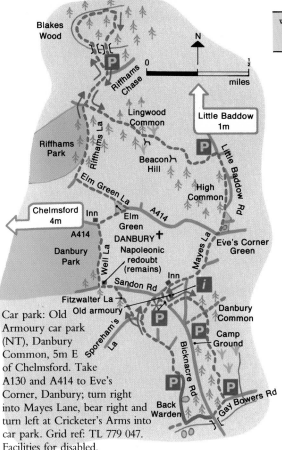

Blakes
Wood

N

Riffhams
Chase

0   ½
miles

Little Baddow
1m

Lingwood
Common

Riffhams
La

Riffhams
Park

Beacon
Hill

Little Baddow Rd

Elm Green La

High
Common

A414

Chelmsford
4m

Inn

Elm
Green

DANBURY †

Well La

A414

Danbury
Park

Napoleonic
redoubt
(remains)

Eve's Corner
Green

Mayes La

Inn

i

Sandon Rd

Fitzwalter La

Old armoury

Danbury
Common

Car park: Old
Armoury car park
(NT), Danbury
Common, 5m E
of Chelmsford. Take
A130 and A414 to Eve's
Corner, Danbury; turn right
into Mayes Lane, bear right and
turn left at Cricketer's Arms into
car park. Grid ref: TL 779 047.
Facilities for disabled.

Sporeham's
La

Camp
Ground

Bicknacre Rd

Back
Warden

Gay Bowers Rd

even more care than usual in these areas, to avoid
disturbing wildlife. On its way north the ramble
follows Riffham's Lane, one of the most attractive
country lanes in Essex.

Park in the NT car park below (south-west of) the
Cricketer's Arms and opposite the Old Armoury,
which dates back to the Napoleonic War when the
common was used as an army camp. The armoury is
owned by the NT and open some weekends, when

◁ *The path from Mission Hall, leading out to the common*

△ *The two deep pools on the Backwarden's southern boundary*

NT goods are available and there is a small exhibition. Danbury Common, once more open with extensive heather heathland, now consists mainly of secondary birch-dominated woodland with gorse and blackthorn thickets. There are some clearings, most of them recently re-created. The common is rich in birds, plants and insects.

Leave the Old Armoury by the lane running south-east and after 25y take the lane-side path. After 15y turn left along the Mission Path and cross Chapel Road at the former Mission Hall to the main part of the common. Proceed past the seat and through the gorse, crossing the main east-west bridleway to the Camp Ground (the main car park). Follow the low bank across the Camp Ground and take the path to the left of the trees, which leads into a grassy clearing. Look out for alder buckthorn, the food-plant of the brimstone butterfly caterpillar. The primrose-yellow males are conspicuous in the spring and late summer.

Keep straight on and then bear left, taking the drier path through the trees to a clearing containing the largest expanse of heather on the common, which is responding well to the NT's bracken-swiping pro-gramme. Admire the little yellow tormentil and other heathland plants, and look out for redpolls. Take the path on the far side of the clearing down to Gay Bowers Road car park, where you turn right along the road and proceed to the junction with Bicknacre Road. Cross over and you are now in the south-east

△ *Lingwood Common's southern slopes, from Elm Green Lane*

corner of the Backwarden part of the common, managed by Essex Naturalists' Trust. The common as a whole is a site of special scientific interest.

The Backwarden nature reserve contains a great variety of habitats, including a number of pools and bogs. Consequently it is extremely rich in wildlife. (A guide to the Backwarden nature trail is available from the Old Armoury or from the Essex Naturalists' Trust, see page 127.) Continue westwards along the path close to the Backwarden's southern boundary, passing a colony of lily-of-the-valley on the left, until twin deep pools rich in aquatic plant life are seen on the left. Walk northwards up the path, almost opposite the pools, which bisects the reserve. Note on the right two heather clearings and the shallow pool between them. As you approach the Backwarden car park look out for patches of the white climbing fumitory.

Take the path to the left at the north-west corner of the car park and turn right on to a north-south path at the reserve's north-west corner. Keep bearing left to arrive at Sporeham's Lane which bisects the Horne Row part of the common. (Walkers wishing to return to the starting point should turn right along Sporeham's Lane and the car park is away to the right.)

Turn left along Sporeham's Lane and after 80y cross the lane and walk up the unmetalled Fitzwalter Lane to Sandon Road. Turn left again and cross the road immediately before the T-junction. This is the extreme north-west point of Danbury Common and you can see traces of an earth redoubt built as a defence measure during the Napoleonic War. At the T-junction turn right and proceed north along Well Lane. On the left is Danbury Park (part Essex County Council Country Park). Danbury Palace, now a management centre, is within the park and was the former seat of the Bishop of Rochester.

At the end of Well Lane cross over the main A414 road with the usual great care to the Bell pub, and turn right to walk up Danbury Hill to Elm Green and its war memorial. Turn left into Elm Green Lane and, some way along, right into the attractive Riffham's Lane. On the left is the parkland of Riffhams and to the right are good views of the south-facing slopes of Lingwood Common.

At the next T-junction bear right into Riffham's Chase (Little Baddow) and continue to the entrance to Blake's Wood car park on the left. This NT wood (also a site of special scientific interest) is managed as a nature reserve by Essex Naturalists' Trust. An undulating and ancient mixed deciduous wood, it is renowned for its spring bluebell display and for other flowering plants. The path follows the valley stream for most of its way and you may see yellow archangel, lily-of-the-valley and early purple orchid.

From the car park take the second path from the right, descend and cross the stream. Turn left and pass a conifer-planted hill on the right. Here look for great woodrush on the slope on the left. Keep bearing right in a large loop as you descend to the stream, listening for the song of blackcap and other warblers. Cross the stream and climb back to Blake's Wood car park.

From the car park entrance turn right back into Riffham's Chase and after 350y go left on to the Lingwood Common approach path (finger-posted *Public Footpath*). Lingwood Common is noted for its birds (including nightingales) and interesting flora, and is another site of special scientific interest. Keep to the main path high up on the common's slopes. On reaching the clearing with a seat among some heather growth, pause to admire the view to the south across to the spire of Danbury Church at the highest point on Danbury Hill (362f). Continue through a cleared grassy area busy with butterflies in summer, and arrive at Beacon Hill (another seat). The imposing views are over Chelmsford to the west and Galleywood to the south-west. Carry on along the main path, noting on the right the giant horsetail, a primitive type of plant, and arrive at the small Lingwood Common car park in Little Baddow Road.

Turn right into the road and when you reach the linear High Common (NT), walk south parallel to the road through the open secondary woodland. Rejoin Little Baddow Road, cross to the east side, and proceed to the crossroads at Eve's Corner, Danbury, with its village pond and small green (NT, managed by Danbury Parish Council). A walk round the pond reveals that the aquatic vegetation includes sea club-rush — a rare plant inland.

Cross to the south side of the main A414 road and then turn right, crossing Mayes Lane at its junction with the A414. From the north-east corner of the sports field enjoy impressive views to the south of the country below Danbury Hill, with Hanningfield Water (reservoir) in the middle distance, industrial Thames-side beyond, and the North Downs of Kent on the skyline. Walk along the west side of Mayes Lane, noting the flower-rich bank that includes meadow saxifrage. Keep bearing right into Pennyroyal Road and finally you are back at the Cricketer's Arms, the Old Armoury and the car park.

◁ *Lily-of-the-valley spreads mainly by creeping, its scarlet berries are uncommon* △

The Trust in London

England's finest Stuart mansion, with its treasures and a restored historic garden . . . the ultimate neo-Classical achievement of Robert Adam . . . a dozen other houses, large and small, important architecturally or with literary associations . . . even 900a of woods and pasture all within the bounds of Metropolitan London. Add a snuff mill at Merton, a sixteenth-century manor house in Barking, a Wren period schoolhouse in the heart of Westminster, a dubiously labelled 'Roman bath' in a basement off the Strand and – across the Thames by Southwark Cathedral – our last remaining galleried inn, and we have an indication of the role the NT plays in preserving our heritage in the capital.

The Trust's open spaces in London survive as islands from the past, amid the encroaching tide of bricks and mortar. They include the 53a of East Sheen Common, adjoining the north side of Richmond Park, and 140a at Osterley Park, where the tree clumps and ornamental water were laid out in the eighteenth century. Petts Wood and Hawkwood provide 330a of rural relief between urbanized Chislehurst and Orpington, while a little to the west, only 3m from Croydon, lies the Trust's 200a Selsdon Wood nature reserve, a haven for plant and animal life.

The most important of the NT's London buildings are Ham House, near Richmond, and Osterley, near Heathrow. The former recalls the years from 1670 when its furniture and pictures were collected. The little 'closet' rooms, intimate with their original furnishings, are especially evocative of the seventeenth century. Osterley, by contrast, is light and elegant. Its architecture, interior details and furniture designs were created a century later than Ham House, by Robert Adam. It takes us faithfully back to 1761–80 when he remodelled the original Elizabethan house into the glittering display that greets us today.

Hampstead offers us Fenton House, with its stunning collection of porcelain and early keyboard instruments. This friendly, welcoming, family house dates from the William and Mary period and is one of the oldest houses in Hampstead. Its walled garden is especially delightful. A taste of Old Chelsea is provided by numbers 97–100 Cheyne Walk, formerly one house, which has retained one of the finest seventeenth-century exteriors in London. Nearby, in Cheyne Row, is Carlyle's House (1708), home of the Scottish historian and philosopher Thomas Carlyle from 1834 until his death in 1881. It is open to view at published times and contains Carlyle's memorabilia.

Although The George Inn at Southwark was built in 1677, it reminds us also of the heyday of the stagecoach towards the end of the eighteenth century. Still a working pub, The George well repays a visit both for liquid refreshment and for a brush with Charles Dickens, who mentions it in *Little Dorrit*.

Close to where Caxton Street meets Buckingham Palace Road, in Westminster, is London's most charming schoolhouse. The Blewcoat School provided education for the poor of the parish from 1709 until 1926. A small, square building, it has the appearance of a life-size doll's house; its warm, rubbed brickwork is enriched with baroque detail, and there is a statue of an eighteenth-century 'Bluecoat Boy' in a niche over the door. Today, restored and framed between lines of pleached hornbeams, the Blewcoat School serves as the NT's permanent London shop.

▽ *The tapestry room at Osterley Park*

Knole Park

A moderate walk in the Kent countryside east of Sevenoaks. The route encompasses the NT's Knole House, close views of this great residence and its gardens, the beautiful Knole Park and superb wide views over the Weald of Kent from a ridge of high ground known as the Greensand Height.

Knole House, set in its 80a of gardens and parkland, is one of the largest private houses in England. But if you can tear yourself away from the house and the delightful acres of Knole Park and the antics of the tame deer, there is plenty of fine countryside outside to explore. This 6m walk takes in Knole Park, woods and farmland, some exclusive residential areas and the high greensand ridge across to Bitchett Green and Godden Green. Because of the deer and other livestock on the way, dogs should be restricted. Also, some short sections of the walk are on bridleways and so mud-proof footwear is essential. If you wish to see the pictures, furniture, rugs, tapestries and silver inside the house remember that the walk takes around three to four hours, so plan your day with care.

Park at the NT's main Knole car park and view the

△ *Knole House, extended in 1603 by Thomas Sackville*

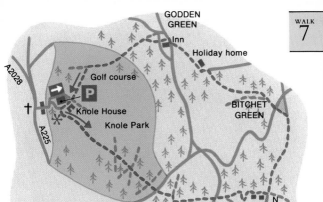

GODDEN
GREEN

Inn

Holiday home

Golf course

P

BITCHET
GREEN

Knole House

Knole Park

A2028

A225

+

N

Car park: Knole
House and Park (NT) on E
side of Sevenoaks, just E of A225.
Grid ref: TQ 531 547.

0   ½   1

miles

great house, home of Lord Sackville. It has 365 rooms
(one for each day of the year), 52 staircases (to match
the weeks) and seven courtyards (for days in a week).

Walk to the outside of Knole House and its
immediate gardens, and head for the south-western
boundary – a long grey wall. Keep this on your left and
follow it round along the farther side of the garden.
Iron gates in the tall wall give an intimate view of the
house at the side. At the end of the wall strike roughly

△ *Leaving Knole Park to enter woodland to the south-east*

53

south-east across the parkland, ever so slightly right of your line of walk. There is the semblance of a path that leads between two trees and crosses a drive. Take the hard path on the other side and ignore a path to the right at a small triangular green. A few yards farther go on the left fork, reach another drive and cross over for a path through trees to a gate out of Knole Park.

Cross the road into a woodland slightly to the left. At a horse-riding paddock head for the top right-hand corner and a stile. Follow the track beyond to the right for a few yards and climb over the stile on the left. The path ahead gives the first of the fine outlooks over the Weald. It comes out on a lane, which you cross and go down a *No through road* on the other side, marked with a footpath stone.

At a fork of paths a little way along you may be lucky enough to see a llama. This long-necked creature, which is a native of Peru, often grazes in the field on the right. Past the llama take the left path up a slope, pass a cottage on the right and turn up the small track to the left of a garage. The path twists and turns before it reaches a small lane. Go left, uphill, ignoring a footpath on the right.

The hard road deteriorates into a very muddy bridleway going up a steep incline. With some relief you find a hard road again at the top. This pleasant

△ *Farmland between Godden Green and the re-entry to Knole*

▷ *Despite its plump, cosy
image, the woodpigeon is the
farmers' number one pest*

leafy way takes you northwards about 300y to the
grassy triangle of Bitchett Green. Turn into the road
on the left, and where it joins another road go straight
across and up the driveway opposite that serves a
number of private houses.

At a fork in the path ignore the signstoned one
going left and continue straight ahead. The path
becomes narrow and more overgrown as it goes
downhill, leaving the houses behind. At a field walk
ahead across a delightful little valley, full of daisies in
summer. Keep going in the same direction past a small
wood on your left. As you go down into a shallow
valley, farther on you will see a stile leading into more
woodland.

Stay on the main track ahead (westwards) and in due
course the path joins a wider way which becomes a
made-up road passing the Mary Mead Holiday Home
on the right. This road joins the public road at Godden
Green, where you turn right. At the end of a row of
cottages beyond the Buck's Head inn go up the road at
the side and past riding stables. At its end you cross over
an unmade road and walk ahead through a gate into
woodland. Immediately inside choose the right fork
which joins a wider track. This leads you, after passing
farmland on the right, to a gate back into Knole Park.
Walk along the hard road through the golf course for
several hundred yards, then through an avenue of fine
trees and back to the Knole House mansion.

As a finale to the walk, go around to the front of the
house and down the made-up road leading away from
it. There are excellent views of the house, and if you
look carefully on the left (south) there is a domed roof
low on the ground among the trees. This is the top of
the ice house, the place where food was stored in the
days before refrigerators.

Scotney Castle

Scotney Castle, south-east of Tunbridge Wells in Kent, is set in beautiful and picturesque landscape gardens. This walk is based at Lamberhurst and meanders through the nearby countryside of parkland, woods, grazing land and the banks of the River Teise on its way to visit the castle and gardens.

Scotney Castle (NT), with its grey fourteenth-century battlements reflected in the water of its moat, is a favourite subject for photographer and artist. You cannot actually see this view from a public footpath, but this 6m walk does cross the driveway which enables you to detour to the castle and its gardens. The majority of paths are through typical gentle Kent countryside, taking in farmland, hop gardens and parks. Livestock is likely to be encountered in the pastures on the way, so do not take your dog and remember to shut all gates securely after you have passed through.

From the public car park by the Chequers Inn in

△ *Finchcocks, at the start of the walk's return leg*

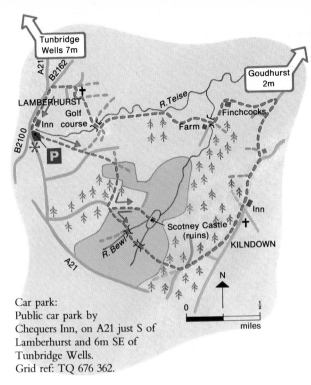

Car park:
Public car park by
Chequers Inn, on A21 just S of
Lamberhurst and 6m SE of
Tunbridge Wells.
Grid ref: TQ 676 362.

Lamberhurst walk away from the main road through
a sporty area. First cross a cricket field, then go through
a hedge gap and cross a football ground. A stile in the
top right-hand corner leads to a golf course. Provided
you can dodge the sport participants and their cricket
balls, footballs and golf balls, walk across the golfers'
grass to find a stile in the right-hand end of a hedge
ahead. Follow the right hedge and fence to a stile.

Ahead, left of a large tree, is a concrete farm road
which you cross by stiles. Make for the hedge ahead
and follow it to the right briefly, then take a track
going up a slope on the left. Keep to the right
boundary all the way to the top and pass through a
five-barred gate on the right. Follow the fence on your
left and, where it turns a corner, continue ahead across
grass through a group of large trees.

The right of way, marked by one or two wooden
posts, goes downhill. Where the paling fence on the

△ *Lamberhurst Church nestles into the Kent landscape*

right turns a corner, carry on ahead for a stile in the right-hand corner. The path goes into woodland ahead and up an incline. Take care near the top because the land on the left side falls away. You emerge on the driveway to Scotney Castle, where a left turn takes you up to view the attractive property. The castle is set in an estate of 782a with the castle as a focus for the landscaped gardens, created by the Hussey family in the 1840s.

On your return from the castle go through the gate on the other side of the driveway. Ahead is fine parkland. Walk half-left, downhill until you pick up gates ahead which take you across a bridge over the tiny River Bewl. Farther on cross another gated bridge and continue in the same line over grass and later a more clearly defined path to a white gate that gives access into woods at the top.

Follow the track until you come to an obvious major junction of paths; take the one to the left, marked by a post. Ignore small side paths and where the main path veers to the left near the top of the incline, continue ahead along a narrower grassy path. At the top you pass a cottage on the left and about 20y farther on, where there is a marker post, go left for a few yards to find a wide way under spreading tree branches going in the same direction. Follow this track out to the public road at Kilndown, the village where the celebrated actress Dame Edith Evans lived. On the right is the church, but you take the lane to the left and walk past the quaintly-named Globe and Rainbow pub (unless you are thirsty and it is opening time).

Past the pub, ignore all footpath signstones on the left of the road for about ½m. Where the road begins to bear right and go downhill, leave it for the track marked with a footpath stone, on the left by a cottage called Hillside. This may be a little overgrown, but passable, in summer. The path soon goes past a cottage on the right, a rough road and then another cottage before reaching a fence at the end. Through the gate, at once use the stile on the right into a pasture. Walk diagonally across to the farthest corner where a gate leads to an estate road serving several properties.

Turn left and you see the splendid red-brick facade of a Georgian house, Finchcocks. Within is a marvellous collection of nineteenth-century pianos and other stringed instruments and organs, which are demonstrated to visitors during the house's opening hours.

The estate road runs alongside this big house and round its back, in a long left-hand loop. On reaching a little bridge over a stream, ignore the wicket gate on

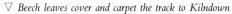

▽ *Beech leaves cover and carpet the track to Kilndown*

the right and instead take the larger five-barred gate immediately beyond. Keep to the right boundary, with the house and buildings of Little Scotney Farm on the rise to the left. At the end of the field climb the stile, made from a step and a short tree stump, into the next field. Go half-left to a gate leading into a hop garden. Follow the path ahead to the gate at the end. In the pasture beyond you should catch glimpses of the tower of Lamberhurst Church, which is now your aim.

△ *Kent hopland from the path below Little Scotney Farm*

Cross the grass diagonally left to find a stile in a fence, hard by the narrow River Teise hidden by trees to your right. The next field is very large and may contain crops; the right of way goes to the top right-hand corner. All the way the river winds peacefully among the trees to your right. Over the stile, go ahead as the land falls away slightly to the right. Keep a row of tall trees to your right. Then follow the Teise as it bears left to find a metal footbridge over the river.

On the north bank of the Teise is a well-marked path north-west to the church. Leave the churchyard for a road with the golf course on your left. Poor putters may have advanced only one or two holes from when you passed on the outward section of the walk. Reaching the main A21 road you have a pleasant walk down the high-level path through the village to the car park.

▽ *The ghost-white barn owl flits past as dusk gathers*

◁ *Hop fruits are harvested on a massive scale in Kent, for flavouring and preserving beer*

△ *The stile and fence near the River Teise, to the right*

Leith Hill

This beautiful walk meanders through the woods and meadowland of the North Downs with panoramic views over to the South Downs from Leith Hill – the highest point in south-east England. Walkers may also explore the Leith Hill Rhododendron Wood, with its many different trees.

Although Box Hill (walk 3) provides some fine views Leith Hill, at 965f nearly twice as high, is a marvellous viewpoint. The surrounding country is chiefly wood-land and some sections of this 6¼m route are muddy in wet weather. The NT owns and maintains several sites in the triangle formed by the A25, A24 and B2126 roads, and this walk takes in most of them. Paths are numerous in this part of Surrey and the route twists and turns in places, so take good up-to-date maps with you. Leith Hill Place contains the famous Rhododen-dron Wood which includes tulip trees as well as rhododendrons and azaleas.

Take the path from the back of the car park, on your left; after a few yards, at a crossing by a bench, turn right on the main track and follow this to Leith Hill Tower at the summit of the hill. Notice the crab apple

△ *The initial climb through mixed woods to Leith Hill Tower*

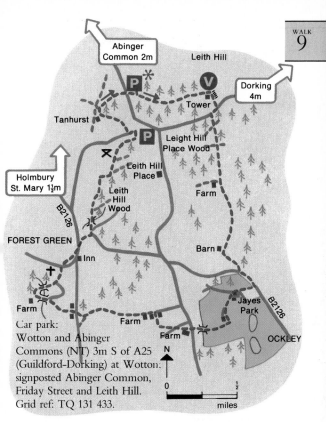

trees and bilberries on your way up. The tower was built in 1776 by Richard Hull, who lived in Leith Hill Place. It brings the height of Leith Hill to 1,029f above sea level, making it south-east England's only 'mountain'. Leith Hill, its tower and Leith Hill Place all belong to the NT. The tower is being renovated and is due to open to the public in the near future.

After looking at the tower and the magnificent views from both sides – you can see the spire of Ranmore Church (walk 11) to the north – retrace your steps. This time keep to your left, with the wooden refreshment hut on your right, and enjoy the magnificent views towards the South Downs as you go. Descend by steps on to a fairly steep path just beyond the viewpoint, and continue down to the road.

△ *Leith Hill Tower: note erosion repair on the approach path*

Turn right on the road for about 50y before turning left into Leith Hill Place Wood, where you take the path from the back of the car park going downhill through wooden posts. At a crossing path keep left and at a further crossing track go straight over to a rough downhill path (signposted). When you reach the foot of the path make for a stile and gate ahead and slightly right. Continue down the right-hand side of the field until you come to the corner of a wood. Here take a diagonal course half-left (south) across the field to a metal gate on the track from Hartshurst Farm. There is a wide view south as you descend the field. Continue on the track, where the hedges are full of wildflowers in summer, and later pass a barn on your right. Here keep left to a road, and then left again on the road towards Ockley.

After a short while take the track on your right by a red pillar box, signposted *Home Farm* and *Jayes Park*. With Leith Hill Tower in view on your right, follow the public footpath sign on an oak tree and cross over a cattle grid; then bear left on to a track and again left at

△ *The panorama across to the South Downs*

the end of the farm buildings. Continue past cottages
on your right; it is worth a backward look along this
track to see the attractive brickwork of walls, turrets
and arches around Jayes Park.

Turn right immediately past the cottages to go
under a loose wire barrier on to a track at the top of a
wire-fenced field. You are now on a permissive stretch
of path. Cross the small bridge and stile in the corner
of the field on to a path, keeping left at a junction, and
negotiate a stile to the road where you cross over and
take the drive opposite, to Volvens Farm.

Continue between houses to the end of the drive
where you bear slightly right to a rough path and on
until you meet a crossing drive. Here maintain your
direction over the drive to a hidden, possibly partly
overgrown, path through trees for a few yards, and
then over a rickety stile to a field – note two small
footpath signs on trees at both ends of this path. Go
across the field to another stile and take the overgrown
path alongside the garden of a house to reach a road.
Turn left and continue on this track past a farm. About

△ *Stile and path between Jayes Park and Volvens Farm*

250y beyond the farm the track bends left by woodland, and where it bends left again with a field opening on your left, look for a small path through trees on your right.

Go over the stile at the other side of the wood into a field where you maintain direction to a small wooden gate, and continue through a white five-barred gate out to the road. Cross over to your right to take a path between a garage and a house, and shortly cross a broken-down stile to head diagonally through two field openings to a concrete track, where you turn left. Carry on over a bridge and, just before reaching the farm ahead, turn right over a stile into a wood; cross a small bridge and another stile into a field. Keep to the hedge on your right for a few yards and then cross a rough stile into woodland. The path crosses yet another bridge and a high awkward stile into a meadow. Continue ahead with a fence on your left, to a stile, and then left to a track down to the road at Forest Green. Those in need of sustenance may care to call at the Parrot Inn before the final section back up Leith Hill.

Cross the road and turn right, making your way over the wide grassy common by the side of the road to a road fork. Here take the Ockley road past a pond and some interesting old cottages, until you come to the NT sign and a gateway where you turn left into Leith Hill Wood. After a few yards, where the broad track bends right uphill, take a smaller path to the left through a hazel grove and over a small bridge until the track bears right; here take the path to your left and stay on it until you pass the NT's *Dingwall Wood* sign on your left, and come to a crossing track. Turn left and shortly the path bears right; take the left-hand path uphill through a shady wooded walk. Where the track passes some open ground on your left you come to a junction with another track, where you keep straight on uphill.

About 10y before the field on your left becomes woodland, take a small path on the right and keep to the lower border of the open woodland area. When you arrive at a gate and fencing on your right, turn left on to a small path in line with the angle of the fencing. Continue uphill until you come to the car park in the Rhododendron Wood. There is a picnic site adjacent to the car park if you have refreshments left.

Continue uphill to the road where you turn left and very shortly right through a small wooden gate to a leafy, enclosed path alongside a private drive. As you approach an open area, with the buildings of Tanhurst on your left and a wide sandy crossing track ahead, take the path above the one you have come on, sharp right and uphill through trees. Continue until you reach the road where a turn left and another almost immediately right will land you back at the start.

▷ *Hazel leaves and cobs (nuts). Hazels are cultivated as well as growing wild*

◁ *The woodmouse dines on hazel and other nuts, and often stores food in a communal larder when supplies are plentiful*

Ashridge

The magnificent Ashridge Estate covers 4,000a of wood and downland on the main ridge of the Chiltern Hills, straddling the borders of Buckinghamshire and Hertfordshire. This beautiful and most instructive walk demonstrates the process of natural reclamation from open downs to mature beech and oak forest, and the route crosses Ivinghoe Beacon and follows a section of the Ridgeway Path.

This $6\frac{3}{4}$m walk combines beautiful and varied scenery with an illuminating insight into the natural process of reclamation. When grazing ceases on open downland the scrub invades and gradually the forest regenerates – beech, oak and several other major tree species are seen. Sections of the walk include the Ashridge Nature Trail, Ivinghoe Beacon (700f) with its excellent views, iron-age hill fort and bowl-barrows, and the Ridgeway Path long–distance footpath. In general the route is firm and clearly marked, but such are the views and the natural history (plus a couple of steepish climbs) that four hours should be allowed.

The walk begins at the Information Centre and opposite the Bridgewater Monument, erected in 1832 in memory of Francis Egerton, third Duke of

△ *The odd-shaped oak, once in a laid hedge, near the start*

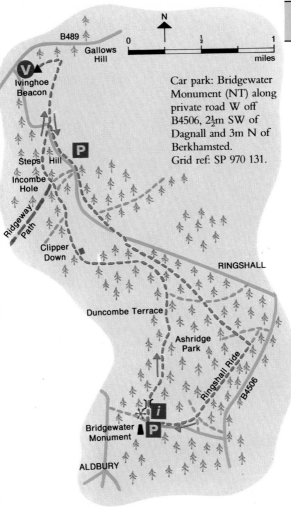

B489

Gallows Hill

0   ½   1
miles

Ivinghoe Beacon

Car park: Bridgewater Monument (NT) along private road W off B4506, 2½m SW of Dagnall and 3m N of Berkhamsted.
Grid ref: SP 970 131.

Steps Hill

Incombe Hole

Ridgeway Path

Clipper Down

RINGSHALL

Duncombe Terrace

Ashridge Park

Ringshall Ride

B4506

Bridgewater Monument

ALDBURY

Bridgewater. The route follows the Ashridge Nature Trail up to point 4, the trail being waymarked by signs and posts with yellow arrows. The initial areas of woodland are comprised of very large beech and oak trees, creating an effect of glades on the forest floor. These sun-dappled glades form valuable habitats for several creatures, particularly the speckled wood butterfly, and where light reaches the ground a covering of vegetation such as brambles and nettles springs up to provide shelter for the smaller mammals.

Continue along the trail and cross a small wooden bridge over what appears to be a gully. This was in fact an ancient trackway marking the county boundary between Hertfordshire and Buckinghamshire. About 80y past the bridge, travelling straight on, notice a peculiar shaped tree. This is an old oak which once formed part of a laid hedge and attained this shape by being allowed to mature. Pass by the right or left side of this tree to reach a small log cabin, once used by the Boy Scouts but now deserted.

Follow the path above the log cabin northwards along Duncombe Terrace. As you stroll along the terrace notice the many tree species including field maple, sycamore, elder, hawthorn, ash, oak, beech and also conifer species such as Corsican pine, cedar and larch. Note also the large sunken pits to the left and right. These are 'dell holes', created in the past by local people extracting the chalk.

As you follow the track north along the scarp ridge the wood starts to fall away to the left. There is little ground vegetation here because of the closed canopy of mature beech trees. This is one of the oldest parts of the woodland and is a typical example of a 'beech hanger'. Farther on is a small plantation of Corsican pine and beech, with the pine planted to shelter the beech during the early part of their lives. As the plantation matures the Corsican pine will be removed, leaving the beech to mature.

The plantation borders on to a scrub area with a magnificent view down the edge of the scarp to the small village of Aldbury. The scrub is predominantly hawthorn and hazel, providing cover for several species of woodland and wood-edge birds. In the summer flowers abound with butterflies: marbled white, wall, meadow brown, small heath, ringlet, small copper, small tortoiseshell and several species of blues, skippers and whites.

Continue past another small plantation on the left and after this the track borders grazed pasture. You wind your way around Clipper Down Cottage and to the left a view opens out across into Buckinghamshire.

△ *The view down the edge of the scarp, towards Aldbury*

The nearest skyline is the Ridgeway Path, which finishes at Ivinghoe Beacon to the north. From Clipper Down you reach a junction in the track; take the right-hand path and follow this until the track begins to rise steadily to the road. Here you find a bridlepath leading along to the left which you follow away from the track.

The walk now leaves mature 'high forest' and exhibits a succession of changes in vegetation, ending with the chalk downland of Ivinghoe Beacon. In fact you are 'walking back in time' since this sequence of vegetation is the exact reversal of the natural process whereby grazed chalk downland reverts back to high forest. Follow the bridlepath until the view opens out. In front you can see Incombe Hole, a striking feature used during the war as a testing ground for munitions.

The Ridgeway Path comes over the stile from the left, and you turn right to follow it to its end on Ivinghoe Beacon. But before you leave Incombe Hole, notice the difference between the 'improved' pasture with added fertilizers on the level surfaces of the hole and the 'unimproved' pasture on the steep sides of the hole. The addition of fertilizers effectively destroys the characteristic downland flowers, replacing them with a monoculture of grass, so that 'unimproved' pasture is far richer and more varied.

△ *Clipper Down Cottage*
▷ *The path descends before
rising to the summit of
Ivinghoe Beacon ahead*

Travel northwards along the track which borders
the fence adjacent to the hole, and eventually the closed
scrub is left behind. As you drop down to cross the
road you can see Ivinghoe Beacon directly ahead. The
problem of erosion caused by thoughtless visitors to
the beacon is highlighted by footpath scars leading
straight up the sides. Walkers should use the
contouring path to the top, to alleviate this problem.
Cross the road and follow this path along the fence on
the right-hand side of the beacon to the top of the
ridge. At the top is a stile; climb it, and to the right the
ridgeline ends at Gallows Hill where a gibbet once
stood. The Icknield Way ancient trackway contours
the hillside here.

Turn left and follow the wide track to the summit of
Ivinghoe Beacon. On a fine day a magnificent
panorama is revealed: eastwards is the large chalk lion
of Whipsnade adjacent to Dunstable Downs, with the
Pitstone Windmill below these to the north.

After a rest to enjoy the views, retrace your steps
back down to the road but instead of crossing over you
should keep straight on south and east along the road
by the path bordering the field edge. This path ascends
gradually to Ivinghoe Beacon car park. Keep to the left
edge of the car park and follow the path through some
large beeches next to the road. This brings you out into

another grassy area, which you cross to follow the path again at the far side. Continue through beech woodland bordering the road and after crossing a track reach a field corner next to the road.

Now you cross the road and follow it south-east for 200y to a grassy parking bay on the right. Over this, take the path leading into the woodland nearest the road. Across the fields to the right is Clipper Down Cottage. Follow the path through predominantly sycamore woodland; this tree does not thrive on the estate since it is readily attacked and often killed by grey squirrels.

Farther along this path, which diverges slowly from the road, you enter yet another type of woodland. This is birch, with its light foliage allowing open areas colonized by bracken. Such habitat is ideally suited to woodland birds, especially the tit family (great, blue and coal), wrens, robins, thrushes and blackbirds. Birch itself is not long-lived but is a successful colonizer of open, heathy areas. In this country it is not generally planted or managed for timber.

Eventually the path intersects a large ride, where if you look left you see a large grassy area. This was once covered in bracken but has been cleared by repeated swiping. This open area is called Ling Rise, due to the traces of heather that can still be found, and is a suitable picnic or rest area.

Cross the large ride and walk through an open stand

▽ *Looking north from Ivinghoe Beacon into Bedfordshire*

of beech trees. Take the second ride on the right, by four large oak trees, before you reach the B4506 road. You are now on Ringshall Ride which leads to Monument Drive and the starting point. As you ramble along the ride there is another species of tree, the sweet chestnut, with its spiral bark and large leaves. Chestnut was at one time coppiced on the estate for fencing, stakes and poles.

The ride dips twice and then rises to a junction where you bend slightly right, noting a twin-trunked hornbeam tree with its small, regular, parallel-veined leaves and smooth grey bark. Hornbeam is not common on the estate; it forms a very hard wood and was used for cogs in mill machinery. You now rejoin the Ashridge Nature Trail, and at point 14 a dew pond is on the left. This part of the estate used to be common land and was grazed by sheep and cattle; the commoners dug out dew ponds to create waterholes for their stock.

Finally you arrive back at the Bridgewater Monument, and for those who still have boundless energy a trip to the top of the monument is recommended.

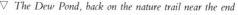

▽ *The Dew Pond, back on the nature trail near the end*

△ *The coal tit frequents pine woods but is seen almost everywhere, especially in winter*
▷ △ *The blue tit feeds high in trees when not at bird tables*
▷ *The long-tailed tit prefers wood edges and clearings*

◁ *The small heath is almost omnipresent but favours grass*
◁ ▽ *The small copper gets through three generations a year*
▽ *Ringlets fly in July and August over lush, grassy scrub*

NATURAL RECLAMATION

The 'typical' chalk downland of short springy turf which botanists enthuse over has been artificially created by humans and their grazing animals; if grazing stops the grass grows ranker, shading out the numerous flowering plants such as orchids and thyme; gradually hawthorn and other scrub plants establish themselves; and eventually they form a closed canopy to shade out and kill the ground vegetation. Meanwhile young trees have established themselves in the scrub, and inevitably they grow over and above the hawthorn. The latter dies away, leaving the semi-mature trees (in Ashridge, oak) to mature.

Polesden & Ranmore

This walk displays to great advantage the
beautiful Surrey countryside north-west of
Dorking, with extensive views to Box Hill
and over the Weald. The ramble passes
through woods, commons and the open
chalklands of the North Downs, a vivid
contrast to the tended borders and terraces of
the gardens in Polesden Lacey Estate.

The Polesden Lacey Estate (910a) and Ranmore
Common (470a) are the main NT sites on this $7\frac{1}{2}$m
walk. The southern section follows the North Downs
Way long-distance footpath, with wide views south
over Dorking and the Weald to include Box Hill and
Headley Heath (walks 3 and 13). Within the main
route is an easy option of $2\frac{1}{2}$m that takes walkers
around the outskirts of Polesden Lacey Estate to give
splendid views of the house in its setting. Inside the
main house (built in 1823, remodelled in 1906) are the
Greville picture collection, tapestries, furniture and
many other works of art.

Leave the car park and cross the lawn in front of the
main house, down the slope bearing left into
Sheridan's Walk flanked by stone columns at either
end. At the end of the walk are views over the valley to

△ *The view from Sheridan's Walk, just east of the start*

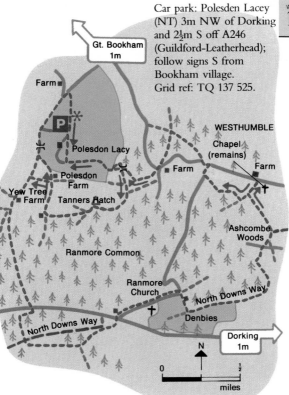

Car park: Polesden Lacey
(NT) 3m NW of Dorking
and 2½m S off A246
(Guildford-Leatherhead);
follow signs S from
Bookham village.
Grid ref: TQ 137 525.

Gt. Bookham
1m

Farm

P

Polesden Lacey

Polesden
Farm

Yew Tree
Farm

Tanners Hatch

WESTHUMBLE

Chapel
(remains)

Farm

Farm

Ashcombe
Woods

Ranmore Common

Ranmore
Church

North Downs Way

Denbies

Dorking
1m

North Downs Way

N

0   ½

miles

Tanners Hatch and Ranmore. Bear right and proceed
down the gravelled driveway to a bridge with a stone
parapet. Do not cross the bridge but turn left on to a
footpath down the bank. Turn right, go under the
bridge and continue along the track. In spring this path
has banks of primroses, violets and bluebells; in
summer it bears a wealth of flowers. Soon the trail
begins to rise, giving views back over to Sheridan's
Walk and Polesden Lacey.

Pause at Tanners Hatch Youth Hostel, to see this
ancient and well-used building which was a very
early youth hostel. Here at the Y-junction, take the
lesser right-hand fork over a stile. Walking uphill, at
the summit look to the right for a lovely view over

△ *The westwards section to Tanner's Hatch, south of Polesden Lacey House; don't forget to close the gate*

△ *Tanner's Hatch, one of the first youth hostels, opened 1945*

Polesden Farm and the southern aspect of Polesden House. Continuing, and shortly uphill again, look for another 'peep' of the house through the trees. Paradise Cottage is just ahead of you. Over the stile at the path end, turn right and drop down to Polesden Farm. (Near the stile at the start of this section is a fine specimen of oak.) Ahead you can see the walled rose garden and some of the fine species of trees standing in the Polesden grounds, with Polesden House in its full glory. On the right look past a stand of copper beeches in the field for views of Box Hill. Go through an iron gate at the end of the path.

For the shorter walk from the iron gate continue ahead along the farm road with Polesden Farm on your right. Walk gently uphill, round a sharp right-hand bend and underneath a thatched wooden bridge that spans the road. At the top of the hill there are

△ *The garden (south) façade of Polesden Lacey House*

extensive views north and west towards London. On a clear day you may glimpse the cream dome of Earl's Court Exhibition Centre in West London. When the metalled road ends, continue onwards down a farm track through the fields of Goldstone Farm, with the grounds of Polesden Lacey on your right. You can see the old stables and the main lodge gate. When a meeting point of several tracks is reached, keep straight on but almost immediately on the right North Lodge appears; cross the green towards it and walk up the main drive of Polesden Lacey and so back to the car park. At the head of the drive, on the left, notice the commemorative plaque to George Mitchell, first secretary of the Ramblers' Association who was connected with many countryside pursuits – including the NT and Youth Hostels Association.

Walkers following the main route turn sharp left after the iron gate, up a concrete road that soon changes back to stony track. Up the hill, noticing the new planting of young trees, there are extensive views down the valley to the North Downs. Over your left shoulder look for more views of Polesden House and gardens. At the top of the rise are Yew Tree Farm and a Y-junction. Keep left and keep left again where three tracks meet quite shortly under a large beech tree.

Proceed up this track for some distance through woods, keeping straight ahead all the time until you meet Ranmore Common Road (metalled) that runs between Dorking and Effingham. Cross this road, turn right and walk a little way along the wide grass verge to a track leading into Forestry Commission grounds (*Forestry Commission* sign). Turn left into the woods. Keep straight on, ignoring any crossing tracks.

The path becomes narrower and a little rougher and eventually drops to the North Downs Way – recognised by a ranch-like fencing gate with the white acorn sign of the Way on it. Turn left (eastwards) through the gate on to the Way. Use the tree-trunk seat here to rest, picnic, photograph or just to admire the wonderful views.

Opposite the tree-trunk seat is a little stile. Go over this into the meadow. Turn left and keep to the track over the downland (ignore all stiles in the hedge) until you reach a large three-step stile at the end of a short rise. This section is of particular interest for the characteristic chalk flowers and butterflies. There are views of Leith Hill Tower (walk 9) on the greensand ridge, Dorking and Westcott in the valley, the Tonbridge–Reading railway line and, on a clear day, the South Downs.

Having climbed the three-step stile into a meadow, follow the path uphill and at the top of the rise take a footpath which bears right towards a copse of trees. Walk towards this copse, skirt it and follow the *North Downs Way* signpost left, over a stile, and again over another stile on to the road opposite a white-painted cottage. Cross the road, walk past the cottage and bear left along the road. Take an inside track along the wide grass verge next to the trees, keeping the road always on your right until a sharp left-hand bend in the road. Here you will pass very close to Ranmore Church – the 'Church-on-the-North Downs Way', with its steeple a landmark for many miles around.

△ *Stile near tree-trunk rest spot on the North Downs Way*

△ *Box Hill dominates the Dorking Gap, seen from Ranmore*

Where the road bends sharply to the left, cross it and turn right. Walk between two large white posts, a white lodge house on your left and into a footpath (signposted *Dorking* and with a North Downs Way acorn sign). Proceed along this track a short way to a farm gate on your right marked *Private* and follow another North Downs Way signpost to the left. You are now on the NT's Denbies Estate. After a short wooded stretch the views continue from the Denbies Estate, there being particularly fine ones of Box Hill. The banks of this track are good for picnics and refreshment stops. Continue along the North Downs Way for some distance, and at a crossing keep straight on. Do not bear right at a track soon after, but almost immediately at a Y-junction leave the North Downs Way and bear left. (Your final North Downs Way acorn post is on the right.)

You are now in Ashcombe Woods, walking past the grounds of Ashcombe House and others on your left. Soon after passing the houses, where the road becomes metalled, there is an optional detour to see the ruins of the old Westhumble Chapel (NT). If you wish to take in the detour, carry on down the metalled road to Chapel Farm and the ruins are on your right. The chapel was founded at the end of the twelfth century for the use of the villagers of Westhumble; it was desecrated three centuries later. In 1937 the chapel was acquired by the NT.

◁ *Ornamental 'copper' beech (shown here with nuts or 'mast') is a variety of common beech*

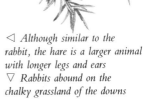

▷ *Junipers are common along the North Downs; the blue-black berries ripen in their second year and are used to flavour gin*

◁ *Although similar to the rabbit, the hare is a larger animal with longer legs and ears*
▽ *Rabbits abound on the chalky grassland of the downs*

Return up the metalled road and where the metalling ends turn right (left if you have not made the detour) up a narrow footpath. Within 20y go over a stile on the right into a field. Walk along the footpath which follows the line of telegraph poles to the field's end, where there are two field gates at angles to each other. Climb over the stile on the left of these gates. From this field are views of The Whites on Box Hill; Mickleham and the Headley Valley leading up to Headley Heath are in the far distance.

Having climbed the stile, the path is narrow-bounded first by a wire-strand fence and then, after a gate, by a hedgerow to the end. Go through the iron field gate on to a road. Turn right down the road, past some cottages to a T-junction, and then turn left with the signpost to Polesden Lacey. Almost immediately after the T-junction, go over the stile at a *Public Footpath* sign on your right. Walk diagonally uphill across the field to a stile at the top, into woods. Continue uphill through the woods until a broad track is reached, turn left along it and continue until it drops down to the left and come out into a field, rejoining the road opposite Bagden Farm.

Walk right (westwards) and shortly turn left into the gravelled drive of the Polesden Lacey Estate. Here there is a flint lodge on the left and a stile on the right of the gate. Once inside Polesden Lacey grounds, follow the gravelled drive all the way back to the car park across the stone parapeted bridge met at the beginning of the walk.

◁ *Marjoram's leaves bear tiny oily glands giving an aromatic scent when crushed*
▽ *The beautiful Adonis blue flies in two generations, in May–June and again in August–September*

Crowlink & Birling

A walk through some of the finest scenery in south-east England, this area has been defined a 'Heritage Coast' in recognition of its exceptional scenic quality. The route is on high chalk country west of Eastbourne and offers magnificent coastal views from the Seven Sisters cliffs, fragrant chalk turf underfoot, pleasant woodland rides, and interesting flint buildings.

This long and lovely 8m ramble is based on the NT's Crowlink site – 632a of cliff, down and farmland including part of the Seven Sisters cliffs. Adjacent to Crowlink on the east side is the NT's Birling Gap, 72½a that form the cliff approaches to Beachy Head. The coastal part of this walk follows the South Downs Way long-distance footpath along the Seven Sisters; the inland sections include the Cuckmere Valley and

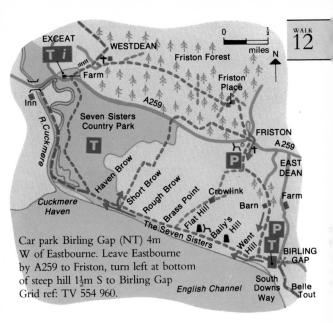

Within the map image:

Car park Birling Gap (NT) 4m W of Eastbourne. Leave Eastbourne by A259 to Friston, turn left at bottom of steep hill 1½m S to Birling Gap Grid ref: TV 554 960.

Friston Forest. Enjoy the walk but please remember to keep dogs under control (most of the route is grazed by sheep or cattle), keep away from the abrupt cliff-edge, and bypass the barriers that have been erected along the coastal path to divert walkers sideways on to less-eroded areas. Also remember that the cliff-top can be cold and breezy even on a fine day, so take enough warm clothes. For those who do not wish to do the full walk, there are shorter alternatives.

At Birling Gap car park there are refreshments, toilets and access to the beach. From the inland side of the car park, take the unmade road west up the hill. From here to the River Cuckmere the route follows the coastal section of the South Downs Way long-distance footpath; follow its waymarks where the path goes westwards on to open downland.

You are on NT land. Looking back, the next hill – capped by the disused Belle Tout lighthouse – is also owned by the NT, as is the hamlet of Birling Gap. Beyond Belle Tout is the higher ground of Beachy

◁ *The third 'sister' of the seven headlands on the route*

85

△ *Looking back to Birling from Flat Hill, sister three*

Head. Cliff falls and erosion by feet make it necessary
to re-route the coastal path periodically. At low tide
you can see the wave-cut platform, all that remains of
the former cliffs.

Shortly you reach the crest of Went Hill – the first
'sister'. Underfoot is rich downland turf, kept short by
sheep, rabbits, feet and the inclement salt spray. Spring
cowslips and violets are followed in summer by wild
thyme, trefoils, bedstraws, salad burnet, milkwort,
various thistles, and many more flowers. Rabbits hop
into the taller thistle patches, and vividly coloured
goldcrests eat the seeds.

On Baily's Hill (the second sister) is a monument to
the Robertson brothers, in whose memory this land
was given to the NT. It is followed by another
memorial stone on Flat Hill, and a seat. In the next
valley you cross the rectangular foundation of a coastal
fortification against Napoleon. Next is a stiff climb up

△ *A view inland from the coastal South Downs Way*

△ *Coming off Haven Brow to Cuckmere Haven*

to Brass Point (sister number four), where you cross into Seven Sisters Country Park which is owned by East Sussex County Council. Rough Brow is number five, and halfway up Short Brow (number six) a stile over the inland fence offers a shorter route. For this short-cut follow the path inland to the main road, cross into Friston Forest, and make your way up to the right, to rejoin the main route at Friston Church.

For the main walk continue along the coastal path to the final and highest sister – Haven Brow – and a magnificent view. In front, beyond Seaford Head, lies the port of Newhaven and you may see the Newhaven-Dieppe ferries picking their way among the coastal shipping. From Haven Brow you continue ahead to drop down to Cuckmere Haven, then follow the track along the foot of the hill and the concrete road up the valley. Cuckmere Haven is one of the few undeveloped river estuaries in south-east England; in past centuries it saw smugglers, coastguards, fisher-men, and a Napoleonic army barracks.

Skirt the brackish meanders of the River Cuckmere, embanked in 1846 to improve navigation. Away from the sea breezes the butterflies become more noticeable, including the common blue and vivid Adonis blue. Ahead the flint buildings of Exceat Farm keep alive the name of the former manor of Exceat, ravaged in the fourteenth century by French raids. The foundations of the manor's church are high on the hill to your right, which is also marked by lynchets (terraces at the boundaries of former fields).

At Exceat Farm on the A259 is the Country Park Centre with a shop, a free exhibition about the area and a *Living World* exhibition of live insects and marine life

WALK
12

87

△ *Sheep graze the downs, bored with the view of Belle Tout*

(entrance fee). Over the Exceat Bridge on the opposite bank of the River Cuckmere (about ¼m) the Golden Galleon inn serves coffee and tea all day as well as meals and bar snacks.

Follow the South Downs Way from the roadside up the steep meadow behind Exceat, and down a long flight of steps into Friston Forest. At the foot lies the pretty flint village of Westdean, its former farm buildings now mostly converted into houses. Keep straight over the road, and shortly bear right. On your left you pass what is said to be the oldest inhabited rectory in the country, with parts dating from the thirteenth century. The church dates from the eleventh century, and opposite it may have stood the Royal Palace of Alfred the Great.

Keep left, up the road into the forest. Stay on the metalled road and bear right beyond the Forester's House (waymarked *Friston*). The wide forest ride is ablaze in summer with the taller downland flowers – greater knapweed, mignonette, crown vetch, sainfoin, and many more. Butterflies include the marbled white.

Friston Forest was planted by the Forestry Commission to safeguard a water catchment. The trees have to contend with thin chalky soils, rabbits and salt-laden winds, and grow only slowly. The main species is beech with various conifers, planted as a nurse crop to protect the young beeches, now being removed.

Keep straight on, over a couple of hills with glimpses ahead of Friston water tower, as far as the tarmac drive of Friston Place. Turn left on to the road and follow it round the gardens; halfway up the hill, take a footpath to the right. With Friston Place below, cross a couple of flint-walled fields that give a taste of the area before it was planted with trees. At the top of the second field there is a view back over the forest to the Cuckmere Valley. A final stiff climb through sycamore woods, passing a reservoir to your left, and you emerge into the noise of the A259 road at Friston.

Cross the main road to the pond and seat. The church is another of Saxon foundation with a fine fifteenth-century timber roof and memorials to the Selwyn family who lived at Friston Place. Note the unusual Tapsell gate, for resting coffins.

Take the road southwards to Crowlink. At the far end of the car park is a map and information board.

Beyond the car park, turn left along the fence. The open plateau of Crowlink was taken into the care of the NT in the 1930s to preserve it from threatened development. The land is downs and pasture, and walkers may roam freely. The turf was in the recent past arable land, yet has few flowers growing in it.

Go through a kissing-gate in the wall alongside a windswept wood. Bear right along the next field, towards a distant barn. Soon you have a good view over Birling Manor Farm to Beachy Head, and back over East Dean, another ancient village but with modern extensions. Keep along the crest, past the barn, and back through the gates above Birling Gap to the path where you began.

◁ ◁ *Cowslip, a spring
bloom of chalk pasture*
◁ *Sainfoin, one of the taller
downland flowers, at over
two feet high*
▷ *Another tallish chalk-
based plant is mignonette*

Chalk

'Our blunt, bow-headed, whale-backed Downs.'

On many walks in this book you can see the lines of chalk hills that are the downs – the North and South Downs, on either side of the Weald, or the Chilterns which are their northern extension. The chalk rock under these hills is too soft for building stone, but it is also porous so that rain soaks harmlessly through the ground, leaving the hills uneroded and standing. The downland valleys and coombes are today dry, apart from 'bournes' that flow after exceptionally wet weather. These valleys were probably carved during the ice ages, by water flowing over the frozen ground.

The origin of chalk takes us back to the age of the dinosaurs, when Britain was under a shallow sea. Over millions of years the remains of minute sea creatures collected on the sea bed, and solidified into rock. Millions of years later these beds were rumpled by the great earth movements that buckled up the Alps. The dome of chalk over the Weald has since been eroded away, exposing chalk, sands and clays as a series of hills and vales, with gentle dip slopes rising to abrupt scarps of the downs north and south.

The hard flints hidden in the chalk have been used in the walls of houses, churches and barns. Earlier, flint was the raw material for stone-age tools and weapons.

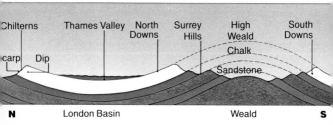

△ *Section through south-east England showing erosion of high chalk over the Weald, leaving the Downs on either side*
▷ *Aerial view of the same area showing surface chalk*

The downs have been farmed ever since those stone-age people first tilled the soil, and they are scattered with the traces of prehistoric tracks, burial mounds and forts, Roman villas and farms, and medieval fields. But the steepest slopes of escarpment and coombe have never been ploughed, and these parts of the downs are famed for their fragrant, springy turf.

When closely grazed, principally by sheep and rabbits, the thin alkaline soils develop an amazingly rich and varied carpet of little flowering plants which supports a corresponding variety of insects. The famous Southdown breed of sheep was reared on this turf, and earlier this century much of the present sea of corn was sheepwalks, where lone shepherds and their dogs tended the flocks.

Parts of the North Downs and Chilterns are well wooded. Here the chalk is masked by clay-with-flints, or gravels deposited by ancient rivers and seas. The clay-with-flints is thought to be the residue of vanished layers of chalk, dissolved away over millennia. But on the bare downs of Sussex and North Kent, it is only man's activity that is keeping the forest at bay. Put away the plough, remove the sheep and get rid of the rabbits, and soon bushes appear, followed by saplings. This process of plant 'succession' (reclamation) can be seen on the steeper downland slopes, where in many places the sheep–grazed turf of 30 years ago is now scrub or young woodland.

The bareness of the downs may be artificial. But, on these hills that '. . . swell and heave their broad backs to the sky . . .', it makes for superb walking country.

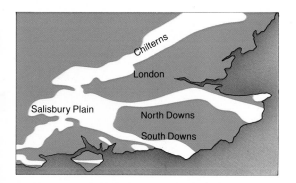

Headley & Box Hill

This varied, pleasing ramble connects two important NT sites north of Dorking – the famous Box Hill, and the 529a of Headley Heath. The soils change from acid heath to Surrey clay, then loam, and finally the chalk of the North Downs; each supports its characteristic plant and animal life. The route includes several fine viewpoints and a section of the North Downs Way.

Allow at least $4\frac{1}{2}$ hours for this $8\frac{1}{2}$m walk, since the countryside is undulating and there is a long, gradual ascent to Juniper Top plus a short, sharp ascent from Betchworth to Box Hill Road. The scenery demonstrates how vegetation changes with the soil type, which in turn is linked to altitude in this part of the North Downs. Be prepared for muddy patches in winter. For those who run out of steam there is a short-cut that trims 3m from the length; for those with limitless energy there is an extra 1m detour to the famous Box Hill viewpoint (see walk 3). The hut at the start provides refreshments and maps of the area.

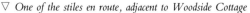

▽ *One of the stiles en route, adjacent to Woodside Cottage*

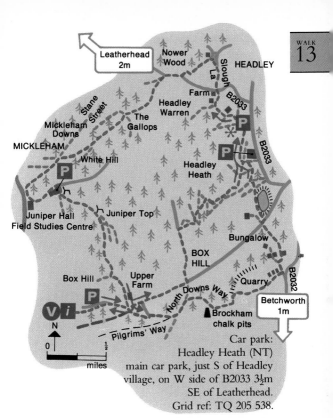

Car park:
Headley Heath (NT)
main car park, just S of Headley
village, on W side of B2033 3½m
SE of Leatherhead.
Grid ref: TQ 205 538.

With your back to the road, leave the car park at the far right-hand corner and continue across the green, keeping the gorse bushes on your right. At a well-defined crossing track with a blue marker turn right and follow the track, avoiding a right-hand turn into a hollow and a ruined cottage. Immediately after passing Goodman's Furze, the large house on your right, take a minor track following the garden boundary fence to the right. Joining a cross track, turn right and head gently downhill, still with the fence on your right. Continue ahead when this becomes a gravel surface, leaving Crabtree Cottage on your left. Shortly you reach a road with Hyde Farm (1830) on your left. Cross directly into Slough Lane (no signpost) passing the late-Tudor Tothill Cottage, and the sixteenth-century Dove Cottage and Slough Farm.

Follow this lane to a junction with a small grassy triangle and bear left, signposted *Public Bridleway*. Almost at once cross a stile on your left, in front of Woodside Cottage, and ascend the gentle slope with a wire fence on your right. The views to the left are of Headley Heath and Little Switzerland. After two more stiles the path continues forward across open meadow to the corner of a woodland, and then follows this round to another stile giving access to a lane. Relish the extensive views including the Mole Gap at Box Hill and Ranmore Church spire on the skyline, before crossing the stile.

Turn left in the lane and shortly you reach the very busy B2033 minor road. Turn right and walk with caution for 200y to the top of the hill. On your left is Headley Warren and to the right Nower Wood, both reserves of the Surrey Trust For Nature Conservation; details are given on a notice board at the entrance to Nower Wood just over the brow of the hill.

Turn left off the road at the *Public Bridleway* signpost and take the left-hand fork south-west along a well-defined track with chestnut paling on one side and an old iron fence on the other. After ½m you see the NT's *Mickleham Downs* sign. This part of the downs is known as The Gallops and contains many species of wildflowers. Along here and in the surrounding area

△ *From White Hill through to Mickleham*

△ *The flint wall and lane after Juniper Hall Centre*

are to be found, in their various seasons, such blooms as rosebay, thyme, viper's bugloss, meadowsweet, restharrow, rockrose, harebell and various orchids. Keep forward along the left-hand side of The Gallops (horse riders are directed along the right-hand side), noting the variety of trees on each side. Far ahead Ranmore Church spire can again be seen.

Towards the end of The Gallops the views open out on the right and at this point bear slightly right to the far right-hand corner of The Gallops, joining a well-defined track on the line of the Roman Staine Street (see also walk 5). Follow this down through the woods and at the bridleway sign bear left, continuing gradually downhill. There are views to the right through the trees to Mickleham, the Mole Valley and Norbury Park. Finally this track runs alongside a redbrick wall and ends in a lane, opposite Juniper Hall Field Studies Centre. Many courses on the countryside are organised from here throughout the summer. At one time the house was occupied by French émigrés and it was here that Fanny Burney met – and later married – General D'Arblay. The house is referred to in her diaries.

At the lane turn left and walk for 600y with a steep wooded hillside on the left and a long, low flint wall on the right. Pass White Hill Cottage to the NT's *Box Hill* sign and small car parking area on the right. This is not the face of Box Hill known to millions but the 'back door' to the famous viewpoint which is still a good mile away. Just beyond the sign is a concrete collecting box and a kissing gate, through which you pass to join the broad track. This ascends the hill south-east to Juniper Top, mainly over open downland. Pause at the second seat for views backwards to Mickleham Downs; in autumn the many colours of dying leaves clothe the steep face of White Hill to the north.

At the top of the long slope – used by winter sports enthusiasts whenever there is enough snow – take the right-hand path of the four well-defined tracks leading into the woods. This leads to a five-barred gate and a kissing gate in the wire fence that otherwise bars your way. Continue ahead, noting the beeches and yews on the right and the reafforestation on the left. Each sapling has its own tubular 'greenhouse' to encourage straight growth and discourage predators such as deer and rabbits. Walk straight on, avoiding all divergent paths, until you reach a major crossing with *Public Bridleway* signs to left and right.

Turn left and follow the clear bridleway. Shortly you have on your left the fence of the Upper Farm Leisure Park (which is in fact a caravan park); eventually you reach the Box Hill Road nearly opposite the Upper Farm Restaurant and Tea Garden, where there is plenty of space for a picnic.

The detour to the Box Hill viewpoint is as follows. Turn right (west) on the road for about 100y to a gap in the car defence bank on the left, and a short track leads through the trees on to open hillside with extensive views over Surrey and Sussex (described in walk 3).

△ *Brockham Chalk Pits scar the southern face of the downs*

Continue along the road to the NT shop and Information Centre, the Zig-Zag Restaurant and Tea Rooms. You must then return to Upper Farm to rejoin the main route.

To reduce the walk by 3m take the short-cut, by turning left (east) along the road from Upper Farm for about ½m to signs *High Ashurst* and *Headley Heath Road*. Turn left and follow the unmade road for ½m to where, beyond the last houses on the right, you find a gate going into Headley Heath. From here it is about 1m back to the car park. There is a multiplicity of tracks across the heath and a general north-easterly direction will bring you to the car park, but make sure your maps and map-reading are up to it.

Those on the main 8½m route should head south from Upper Farm on the well-defined track going downhill. In 100y the acorn signs to left and right signify you are now on the North Downs Way long-distance footpath. Take a left turn and follow the way to the far side of Betchworth Quarries at the foot of the downs. All the way the path is well-marked with its acorn symbols or signposts. It winds through mixed woodland on the face of the downs, passes above Brockham Chalk Pits and descends through the abandoned workings of Betchworth Chalk Pits. Note in passing the grave and memorial to *Quick 29.9.36– 22.10.44 'An English Thoroughbred'*, as well as the many glimpses of the Weald and South Downs through the trees on your right.

△ *Aiming north across Headley Heath, near the walk's end*

△ *Viper's bugloss likes chalk*   △ *Meadowsweet*

Where the North Downs Way enters a rough road
lined on its left with cottages, follow this to a junction
signed *Public Path* and then turn left. Follow the lane
round to the right and at the entrance to two houses,
Highlands and Lynchets, take the footpath on the left
between a private garage and a fence. Just beyond the
end of the fence, pause briefly for your last look back
over the Surrey and Sussex Weald.

At a junction of paths in front take the left-hand side
of the chalk hummock, continuing straight up the
hillside. At the top is an area of scrubland, and to the left
a large fenced field with a solitary bungalow in view.
Keep these on your left and continue ahead to the road.
Turn right and in 80y, immediately beyond a private
entry to Duke's Wood, take the footpath to the left
outside the boundary of the drive to the house. The

△ *Gorse thrives on light soil*   △ *Broom picks lime-free areas*

retaining bank of Headley Reservoir is in front.

The path continues along the left of the reservoir boundary and shortly comes out on to Headley Heath at a major crossing track. The heath was originally extensive sheepwalks until around 1882; it remained mainly open heathland until the topsoil was disturbed by army manoeuvres in the Second World War. After this, scrub reinvaded and birch became established.

Go across the crossing track and bear right. At the first junction turn left and in a few yards right again on to a dirt path. Follow this to a major intersection with Brimmer car park away on your right, and a *No Horses* sign. Here turn left, crossing another clear bridleway, and at once take a parallel footpath which shortly brings you back to the Jubilee Plantation and your car park.

Winkworth

Winkworth, with its famous arboretum, is the
base for this extremely varied woodland and
farmland walk through the greensand tracks of
West Surrey, near Godalming. The route joins
three NT properties: Winkworth itself, a small
site in Hambledon village, and the viewpoint
of Hydon's Ball Hill.

Despite its 8½m length, this ramble gives good walking
in all weathers, partly due to the well-drained sandy
tracks based on the greensand ridge that covers this part
of Surrey. In fact a 2½m section of the walk follows the
Greensand Way long-distance footpath. There is an
enormous variety of woodland habitat and plenty of
views, especially from Hydon's Ball (593f). Plan the
day so that you can include a visit to the famous
Winkworth Arboretum before or after the main walk.

The arboretum itself is a 99a hillside planted with
rare trees and shrubs. There are two lakes, a grassy area,
views over the North Downs, and a selection of walks
in the grounds as described by the leaflets available at

△ *The mixed woodland beyond Longhurst Farm*

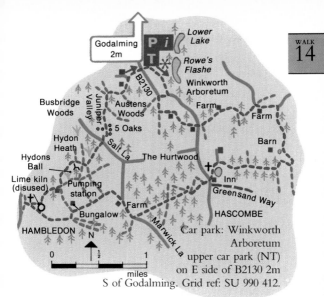

Godalming
2m

Lower
Lake

*Rowe's
Flashe*

Winkworth
Arboretum

Busbridge
Woods

Austens
Woods

Farm

Farm

Hydon
Heath

5 Oaks

B2130

Juniper Valley

Salt La

The Hurtwood

Barn

Hydons
Ball

Lime kiln
(disused)

Pumping
station

Inn

Greensand Way

Bungalow

Farm

HASCOMBE

HAMBLEDON

N

Marwick La

0   ½   1

miles

Car park: Winkworth
Arboretum
upper car park (NT)
on E side of B2130 2m
S of Godalming. Grid ref: SU 990 412.

the NT shop and Information Centre. Spring and
autumn are particularly good times to visit here, for
the beautiful blossoms and the riot of leaf colours.

Starting from the upper car park, face the arboretum and turn right by the donation box. Follow the
public footpath along the property boundary to the
road. Turn right into the B2130 road and after 180y
turn left at a sharp corner. Continue south on the
metalled track and take the first turn left. As you pass
Winkworth Cottage the track bears right by brick
wall; then past Chapel Cottage you descend a gully to
the B2130 road by Yew Tree Cottage.

Cross the road and keeping in same direction pass
through a gate at the crossing track and go half-left at
the second gate, heading north-east. Keep to the track
past Langhurst Farm to enter mixed woodland.
Follow the track as it climbs through the wood and,
just after the field fence appears on the left, the
direction bears right for 20y to meet another track
coming in from the right. Turn left here and descend
all the way to the narrow road. Owls are occasionally
seen in daylight along this section.

Turn right on to the road and notice the old brick
granary standing on saddle stones in the garden of

△ *Looking north-west on the eastern section before Hascombe*

Scotsland Farm. From the farm gate walk about 300y along the road and turn right at the bridleway sign, through a wide iron gate to follow the track with views across to the North Downs. After passing the entrance to New Barn and a pond on the right the track rises slightly. At the top of the rise leave the track to take the sharp hairpin bend to the right (westwards). The path climbs more steeply now, through a gate and into the wood.

Follow the bridlepath where it bears left and soon a deep depression appears on the right. Where the hill levels out at the next junction turn right (west again). Follow the path, admiring the views on the right to St Martha's Chapel on the North Downs, to emerge by the old school at Hascombe village. Pass a pond on your left with its water-lilies, moorhens and Canada Geese, and cottages with their unusual porches. St Peter's Church on the right has a wooden steeple, and the wall of nearby Church Cottage shows a sample of garneting where the mortar joints are decorated with small pieces of black ironstone. At the end of the road you join the B2130 again at the White Horse Inn.

The next 2½m of your route follows the Greensand Way, a long-distance path that runs 55m from Haslemere in West Surrey to Limpsfield on the Kent border. The footpath was inspired by Geoffrey Hollis, who opened the middle section of the route at a ceremony held at Leith Hill (walk 9) in June 1980.

Cross the B2130 Godalming–Dunsfold road and climb the stile into the meadow, to make for the next stile by a water trough. Continue on rising ground and enter the trees of the Hurtwood at another stile. Over this the path bears right and climbs steeply to bear right again at the next track. Continue climbing steadily with a steep drop to your right, and a sunken path comes in on the right. Where the ground levels out turn sharp right for 25y to a wooden post. Turn left at the post and, ignoring crossing tracks, continue to the next road, Markwick Lane.

Turn right along the road to Little Burgate Farm at the first bend. Turn left at this farm and keep to the track with the farm buildings on your left. The views from this sandy track are to Blackdown, Hambledon Hill and Hydon's Ball to the north-west. At Maple Bungalow turn left and then right to Hambledon.

You arrive at the beautiful Hambledon Church, where the NT owns 2½a nearby. The church has a wooden steeple and in the churchyard stands a yew, of course – but an exceptional one that has a hollow trunk said to be large enough to accommodate 12 people. Thirsty walkers may wish to visit the Merry Harriers inn, by taking the nicely-cut grass path which forks right by Stable Cottage gate and winds downhill to the road and pub.

▷ *St Peter's Church, Hascombe, roughly at the walk's halfway point*
▽ *Hascombe's cottages with their unusual porches*

From Hambledon Church take the footpath east-wards along the side of the churchyard, with the wall on your left. On the right is the entrance to a disused lime kiln supposedly in use until the nineteenth century. Pass through one kissing gate and take the diagonal field path to the next kissing gate, then to a third kissing gate in the far corner by an old barn. The path now bears right through a chestnut coppice to meet crossing tracks by a water-pumping station. Turn left at this station into the NT site of Hydon Heath and climb to the summit of Hydon's Ball.

Hydon Heath and Hydon's Ball are 125a of heath and woodland given to the NT in memory of Octavia Hill in 1915. A pause at the memorial seat allows a look at the views and a ponder on the rhyme:

> 'On Hydon's top there is a cup
> And in that cup there is a drop
> Take up the cup and drink the drop
> And place the cup on Hydon's top'

(From *Highways and Byways in Surrey* by Eric Parker.)

From the summit pass to the left of the seat and immediately fork right behind the seat, to head eastwards. As the gradient evens out cross a main track to pass between posts; the path then bears slightly left

△ *Walking north-east through coppiced chestnuts to Salt Lane*

(north-east) to another main track. Cross over this also and continue on a somewhat indistinct path that bears half-right. After about 50y you arrive at the corner of a chestnut coppice. Here fork left to enter the coppice on a north-easterly bearing and continue to Salt Lane.

Cross Salt Lane to a track as it bears left into Busbridge Woods. At five fine oak trees fork left (northwards) and follow the path through coppice, descending to meet a built-up forestry track in Juniper Valley. Continue in the same direction for 55y then leave the track to fork right uphill on a horse track. This emerges from the wood and becomes a narrow path before reaching the metalled road at The Cottage. Keep on in the same direction to a road, where you turn right after the gateposts. Finally you reach a road and you are opposite the Winkworth car park once again, with the tea-room beckoning.

▷ *The tawny owl is a silent nocturnal predator. It hunts in or near mature woodland, swooping on prey from a perch*

△ *The blossom 'candles' of horse chestnut erupt in April and May*
▷ *Sweet chestnut, like its namesake, grows well in the Winkworth area*

105

Ditchling Beacon

For this walk along the crest of the South Downs north of Brighton try to choose a clear day – there are glorious views north, far into the Weald, and south across the downs to Brighton and the sea. The route is mainly through rolling cornfields, with a wealth of downland flowers in summer, and the hill forts, burial mounds and ancient fields recall the long history of this landscape. Much of the route follows the South Downs Way.

Ditchling Beacon, at 813f, is the third-highest point on the South Downs and the views are magnificent. This $9\frac{3}{4}$m route provides ups and downs, chalk, grassland, small Sussex villages and a wealth of wildlife as it connects the two NT sites of the Beacon itself and Newtimber Hill 4m to the west. The section along the South Downs Way long-distance footpath is waymarked; the rest has to be traced with care. The paths are generally firm underfoot, but with muddy patches after rain. Part of the return retraces the

△ *Views north from the route, into the Sussex Weald*

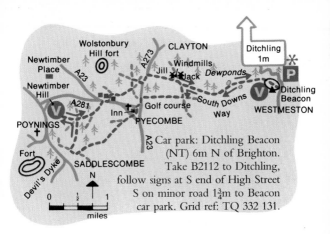

Wolstonbury
Hill fort
CLAYTON
Newtimber
Place
Ditchling
1m
A23
Windmills
Jill
Jack
Dewponds
A273
Newtimber
Hill
A281
South Downs
Way
Golf course
Ditchling
Beacon
WESTMESTON
POYNINGS
Inn
PYECOMBE
A23
Fort
SADDLESCOMBE
Devil's Dyke
N
0   ½   1
miles

Car park: Ditchling Beacon (NT) 6m N of Brighton. Take B2112 to Ditchling, follow signs at S end of High Street S on minor road 1¾m to Beacon car park. Grid ref: TQ 332 131.

outward walk, and those wanting a shorter one-way walk (5¾m) can finish at Poynings, below Newtimber Hill, where public transport is available.

The walk starts at Ditchling Beacon car park, which together with 4a of surrounding land is owned by the NT. The first section is along the South Downs Way westwards; follow its signposts. Take the path from the car park up to the beacon. On a clear day you can see the wooded hills in the heart of the Weald (an Anglo-Saxon word meaning 'wood'), and Leith Hill

△ *Heading west on the South Downs Way*

△ *Arable fields near Newtimber Hill*

(walk 9) beyond. Below lies the village of Ditchling, a centre for artists and craftsmen. To the east are the Ouse Valley and Firle Beacon beyond.

The chalk grassland of the beacon is a nature reserve of the Sussex Trust for Nature Conservation. In spring and summer the entire walk is carpeted with a wealth of downland flowers – from tall knapweeds, thistles and scabious, through the shorter orchids, cowslip, harebell, crested cow-wheat and yellow-wort, to prostrate bedstraws, dwarf thistle and salad burnet. Overhead are the ever-vocal skylarks; yellow-hammers on fenceposts and bushes chorus 'a little-bit-of-bread-and-*no*-cheese'.

Beyond the beacon you cross an indistinct bank which is the remains of an iron-age hill fort. This hill-top track is a very ancient one. The maps show it lined with prehistoric burial mounds, but you will have difficulty spotting any – they have been virtually obliterated by modern ploughing. Along the plateau you pass a couple of dry dew ponds, created to water the sheep pastured here in the eighteenth and nine-teenth centuries. The sheepwalks are now replaced by endless cornfields stretching away to Brighton.

After 1¼m you scale a crest and start the descent to Pyecombe, set among rolling hills. In front is Wolstonbury Hill, with another hill fort; to its left, the wooded slopes of Newtimber Hill. There are glimpses of the famous 'Jack and Jill' windmills (see below) but the South Downs Way turns left just above them to cross Pyecombe golf course. Beyond the main road continue on the South Downs Way up the lane into Pyecombe, where the little flint-built Norman church with its unusual lead font is worth a visit. The house opposite the church used to be a smithy, and earlier a crookmaker's workshop – Pyecombe was noted for its shepherds' crooks. Rejoin the South Downs Way and follow it down the lane to the noisy A23 road, where there is a pub for those with a thirst.

Beyond the main road you start the long haul up Newtimber Hill, through arable fields. There is a fine view when you finally reach the crest. Southwards are the tower-blocks of Brighton, and the 1920s and 30s housing estates whose spread across the downs was one of the spurs to planning legislation. On the open hilltop above the housing is another hill fort, Hollingbury. Turning ahead the view includes yet another hill fort, above Devil's Dyke. This cleft in the downs may have been carved out in the ice ages by streams flowing over frozen ground.

Beyond the crest you enter the NT's 238a of Newtimber Hill. Follow the path down towards the hamlet of Saddlescombe, in the middle ages a community of the Knights Templar. Just before the hamlet, turn right (northwards) into a pasture; keep along its lower edge, up the coombe (valley set in the hillside). On the opposite side of the coombe, terraces indicate ancient fields. Follow the fence line up the hill at the head of the coombe. Turn left through the hunting gate on the hilltop.

Newtimber Hill has been invaded by bushes and brambles, and the NT is clearing the hilltop to restore it

▽ *The lowlands seen from the path to Saddlescombe*

△ *The magnificent scene from the summit of Newtimber Hill*

to grassland. Keep along the plateau to the western end of the hill for a magnificent view westwards along the downs escarpment to the Adur valley and Chanctonbury Ring beyond, with the village of Poynings below. Newtimber Place, a moated Tudor house, lies just out of sight round the hill to the right.

Retrace your steps back along the hilltop to the hunting gate, then keep left above the wood to another gate in the corner of the field. Follow this sunken bridleway down to the valley. Along the lower part, a high bank on the left indicates an old field boundary, overgrown with typical downland shrubs such as sloe and traveller's joy. Reach and carefully cross the main A23 road, and follow a footpath through a gate in a flint wall and then through a yard and across a stile into a field. Climb the field diagonally to the right, to a stile. Carry on up the same line and across another stile; up and over the shoulder of Wolstonbury Hill, and down to a stile. Turn left on to a bridlepath, and shortly right along another, down to the A273 main road.

Cross the road and turn left, keeping to the verge as far as a lane to the right. Leading between hedges for a change, the lane takes you up past 'Jack and Jill', the two windmills. Nowhere else in England is it possible to see two windmills standing side by side. 'Jill', the lower (post) mill, was moved here from Brighton in about 1851, and ceased grinding in 1909; it is open to the public on summer Sundays. 'Jack', the tower mill, was built in 1866 and ceased working in 1908.

Above the windmills, the route rejoins the South Downs Way. Retrace your steps and admire the views for the 1¾m back to Ditchling Beacon and return to the car park.

△ *A stile guides walkers along Wolstonbury Hill*

◁ *Female chaffinch lacks
the male's bright colours*
▽ *Female greenfinch is
also duller than the male*

◁ ◁ *Crested cow-wheat,
beautiful and uncommon*
◁ *Yellow-wort, another
chalk plant*

Traveller's joy ▷

111

Coldrum & Trosley

An ancient burial ground, the NT's Coldrum Stones and long barrow make an interesting excuse for this strenuous but marvellously scenic walk along the scarps and foothills of Kent's North Downs, north-west of Maidstone. Part of the route follows the historic Pilgrim's Way and another section winds through Trosley Country Park on the chalk crest of the downs.

This 11m walk involves climbing and descending the escarpments of the North Downs in Kent, so it can be classed as strenuous. Compensation comes from the splendid views of the line of hills making up this Kent feature, and the rolling farmland below. Kent County Council has set up a major country park, Trosley, on the crest of the downs which makes a convenient starting place. The countryside is high and open in places, so be prepared with good maps and weather-proof garments.

Start the walk along the wide woodland path to the left of the park's Information Centre. After about 200y

△ *Coldrum Stones, scattered memorials to an ancient burial*

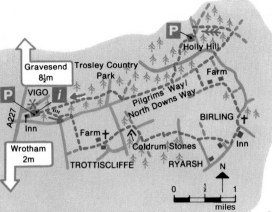

Car park: Trosley Country Park, signposted on E side of A227 Wrotham-Gravesend road, near Vigo Inn 2m N of Wrotham. Grid ref: TQ 634 612.

take the track downhill to the right, which eventually becomes a series of rustic steps. At the bottom do not go through the barriers to the road, but instead follow the track round to the left. After another 200y pass through barriers on the right to reach a stile on the other side of a narrow lane. Over this, follow the right-hand boundary of the field. To the left (north) you have a magnificent view of the downs as they sweep towards the sea.

After another stile to reach an open field, follow the line of electricity wires overhead to the end of the field. Head left towards the clearly-seen Trottiscliffe (pro-nounced Trosley) Church. In the porch of the church are preserved a few of the remains of 22 humans discovered at Coldrum Long Barrow when it was excavated in 1910 and 1922. After passing through a farm complex by the church – an area reminiscent of the corner of a French village – leave the road by a footpath on the far side of a cottage to the left. There is a stile a yard or two up the slope; over this, keep to the left boundary for a stile at a lane lined with dwellings. Cross over and join the track between bungalows.

After some trees the path runs into a field. Follow the right-hand side and at the end you veer right to join another path. A few yards along a concrete path are the NT's Coldrum Stones, where it is thought a local king

△ *Fir plantations at the foot of the downs, near Birling*

△ *The farm track heading back up the downs from Birling*

or chieftain was buried perhaps 4,000 years ago. The 'long' barrow is in fact almost square, about 60f by 70f. The stones that once formed a colonnade around the boundary have fallen; some in the south-east corner have gone, and others along the eastern side have slipped down the slope.

Continue down the hard road, away from the downs. After 100y along, before the bend in the road, take the grassy path going off to the left. The path veers left; ignore a stile soon reached straight ahead and instead turn left into a field, following the boundary.

Where the trees end, continue on the same line through a small field to a stile and over into woodland. Another stile takes you through a pasture. The right of way crosses to a stile just short of the right-hand top corner after which you walk left, with the barbed-wire fence on your left, into woodland. Note the fine group of tall firs on the right. Emerging into a lane, walk to the right and immediately fork left. The lane bends to the left and where it twists to the right, by dwellings, look for a street light on a pole. Here take the farm track on the left.

After 20y, ignore the stile and footpath to the left and continue ahead. In the big field at the end go right, with the fence on your left, to a stile. Follow the left-hand field boundary to another stile. Make for the right-hand end of the hedge running across in front of you, and follow it round to the corner of the field. A

△ *The Pilgrims' Way below Holly Hill*

△ *Climbing the face of the downs towards Holly Hill*

△ *Woodland far below, at the foot of the downs at Holly Hill*

couple of stiles close together take you into a large field.
Go diagonally across, aiming roughly for the house, to
find an exit into the road. On the road turn left and
stroll along to the village of Birling. As usual there is
the pub, then the church; about 150y past the church
take the wide farm track to the left, going back
northwards towards the North Downs.

At a concrete road ignore the spur to the right and
follow the hard road through a farm complex. At the
top of the slope, about 150y past a cottage called
Waggoners and over on the right, go up the track to
the right. At the next T-junction you encounter the
famous and historic Pilgrims' Way, immortalised by
Chaucer, that led medieval pilgrims from Winchester

△ *A sparrowhawk, nimble woodland hunter, feeds its nestlings*

116

to Thomas à Becket's shrine in Canterbury Cathedral. For parts of its route the Pilgrims' Way coincides with the North Downs Way long-distance footpath.

Turn right and at a lane cross over for the continuation of the track slightly to the left. After about 600y look for a public footpath signstoned on the left, and follow it over the stile and up a slope through trees and past a cottage. At the top of the ascent the path goes through trees for about 400y and then enters more open ground with grass underfoot. After a while it climbs very steeply indeed up the face of the downs. Through woodland at the top, a stile takes you into a field where you follow the right-hand boundary – still going uphill. Leaving the field, continue on a track over a drive to a lane. Turn left and in 200y Holly Hill car park is on the right.

Cross the car park in a half-right direction up a slight slope into trees. This pleasant woodland path winds for about $\frac{1}{4}$m to a lane. Cross over to reach a track into trees a few yards to the right. This takes you down the steep wooded escarpment of the downs, a mysterious dark way with dense overhanging branches and tree roots strangely shaped by erosive forces.

At the T-junction of paths at the bottom, take the right-hand one. A good $\frac{1}{2}$m along, where the soft track becomes a hard service road for dwellings, take the North Downs Way (marked by its acorn symbol and signstone) up a steep slope on the right. Near the top of the slope on the left is the entrance to Trosley Country Park. Re-enter the park and follow the woodland track for the final mile back to the car park.

△ *The ravages of Dutch Elm fungus, and the beetle carrying it*

117

Devil's Punch Bowl

This beautiful ramble winds through several extensive NT properties clustered around Hindhead and Haslemere on the borders of Surrey, Hampshire and West Sussex. It is a full day's walking but the wealth of views, varied woods and greensand areas of open heath make the effort well worthwhile.

This walk connects NT holdings at Hindhead Common (over 1,000a, including the Devil's Punch Bowl and Gibbet Hill), Grayswood Common, Stoatley Green and Blackdown. The full walk is 14m (allow at least seven hours) but this can be split into two parts of approximately 8 and 9m by using a path from Imbham's Farm to Haslemere through the NT's Swan Barn estate (details below).

It is a fairly strenuous walk: proper clothing and a good map are essential, and a compass is useful. Most of the walk is over heath and woodland of the lower greensand, except where wealden clay surfaces near Imbham's and Ansteadbrook. Also on the route are sections of three nature trails: the Punch Bowl, Gibbet Hill and Blackdown (see page 120). The NT has

▽ *The dramatic sandstone valley of the Devil's Punchbowl*

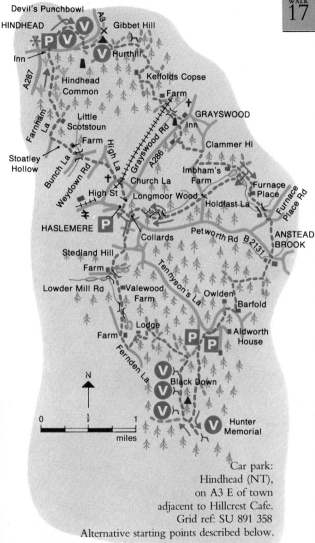

Devil's Punchbowl
HINDHEAD
Gibbet Hill
Hurthill
Inn
A287
Hindhead
Common
Keffolds Copse
Farm
GRAYSWOOD
Inn
Little
Scotstoun
Farm
Clammer Hl
Farnham La
High La
Grayswood Rd
A286
Imbham's
Farm
Furnace
Place
Stoatley
Hollow
Bunch La
Weydown Rd
Church La
Holdfast La
Furnace Place Rd
High St
Longmoor Wood
ANSTEAD
BROOK
HASLEMERE
Petworth Rd
B2131
Collards
Stedland Hill
Farm
Tennyson's La
Owlden
Barfold
Lowder Mill Rd
Valewood
Farm
Lodge
Aldworth
House
Farm
Ferdenden La
Black Down
Hunter
Memorial

N

0 ½ 1
miles

Car park:
Hindhead (NT),
on A3 E of town
adjacent to Hillcrest Cafe.
Grid ref: SU 891 358
Alternative starting points described below.

prepared leaflets describing these trails in full; if the walk is divided into two parts it may be worth following the complete trails. For such a long walk in such a rich area, it is important to lay careful plans.

Leave the A3 car park in a north-easterly direction, past the nature trail notice, for the edge of the Devil's Punch Bowl. There are good views into this dramatic sandstone valley, which shares its attribution to the Devil with other impressive natural features like the Devil's Dyke and Devil's Jumps. Turn right and follow the 'rim' of the bowl to point 2 of the nature trail (orange markers) and another viewpoint, where an indistinct path to the right leads up to the main A3.

Cross this very busy road with great care, then turn left to points 1 and 2 (marked in white) of the Gibbet Hill nature trail. This follows the old road from London to Portsmouth, an historic coaching route, to a stone commemorating the brutal murder of an unknown travelling sailor in 1786; the murderers were dealt with as described below.

So far the walk has been through mixed woodland including rowan, holly, whitebeam, birch, hawthorn, oak and pine. Take the next path on the right to the open space of Gibbet Hill. This is the second-highest point in Surrey, 895f to Leith Hill's 965f. A direction finder identifies the extensive views to Leith Hill, Chilterns, Hog's Back, Weald and Blackdown. A Celtic cross stands on the spot where the sailor's murderers hung in chains from the gibbet which gave

△ *Another view of the bowl, with its mixed woodlands*

△ *Looking down from Gibbet Hill*

the hill its name, and this event added to the awesome reputation among eighteenth-century travellers of the heath as a haunt for outlaws and highwaymen.

Leave Gibbet Hill to the south-east, past point 3 on the trail, and follow this downhill to point 5, a junction of six paths. Take the third from the left, straight ahead and gently upwards to follow an old forest boundary along Hurt Hill, reaching the edge of the escarpment near a seat and NT sign. Go ahead through a group of pines, then veer to the right; continue roughly south, steeply downhill through a chestnut coppice. At the bottom turn right on to a bridlepath, keeping a Forestry Commission plantation on the left, towards Keffolds Copse.

Pass in front of the house and after 300y turn sharp left to wind downhill on a wide lane for 600y to a stile on the right. There take the indistinct path south-east across a field, a crossing track, and two more small fields to the railway. Go over with care. Maintain the south-easterly direction down through woods to a footbridge, then climb to reach the Grayswood Road (A286) near the Wheatsheaf Inn.

Turn right along the road to a war memorial, then cross with caution to the NT's sign for Grayswood Common. Take the small path which turns into an access lane for houses. Opposite Rose Cottage double back briefly to the left, uphill, to take an enclosed path to the right. In June there are magnificent views of many-coloured rhododendrons. This path turns east across fields to reach the road at Clammer Hill. Turn

△ *Trees cloak the sombre slopes of Gibbet Hill*

right along the road for 400y, then go left on to the bridlepath through fields and woodland to Imbham's Farm. You are now in agricultural land, on wealden clay, and the paths can be muddy. Oak, ash, beech, sycamore, chestnut and alder are among the tree species hereabouts.

Imbham's Farm is a much altered sixteenth-century house, with barns of the same era, on the site of a moated medieval manor. It was an important centre of the Wealden iron industry in the sixteenth and seventeenth centuries, under iron-founders named Quenell – a fact reflected by nearby place names of Furnace Moor and Furnace Place. The two large artificial ponds were the sources of power.

Walkers who wish to split the route into two should take the short-cut as follows. After Imbham's Farm turn right to take a path along the dam of the more northerly of the two ponds. Continue on this path roughly south-west, keeping a stream on the right, to cross Holdfast Lane. Maintain your direction through the NT's Longmoor Wood (or make the waymarked detour across the stream and back by two footbridges). Pass the NT's Hunter Basecamp, which provides accommodation for conservation volunteers, and reach the B2131 Petworth Road at Collards, an interesting sixteenth-century house. Here you pick up the return leg of the route, as described below.

Walkers on the full 14m route should maintain a south-easterly direction after Imbham's Farm, leaving

△ *The route through the woods on Hurt Hill*

the two large ponds on the right. Ignore tracks to the left and right as the path becomes the drive to Furnace Place. Near the drive of Stream Cottage a newly waymarked path on the right leads over fields to the junction of Furnace Place Road and a cart track. Turn up this track for about 30y then go right where a fence leads off southwards, with a large field on the left and smaller ones on the right. The apparent right of way is obscured by fencing; the practice in recent years has been to keep the fence on the right until it changes direction and then make for a pole transformer, hence to a field gate near the inside of a bend in the Petworth Road (B2131) at Ansteadbrook.

Cross the road to a bridlepath to the left of Brook Cottage, which after 400y leads to a signposted footpath on the right. Follow this over fields and through a wood uphill to reach a bridlepath. Turn left and walk on to reach Tennyson's Lane at Barfold, then right and up this steep and narrow sunken road. After 300y, on the inside of the bend opposite the entrance to Owlden, take a distinct path to the left (not shown on OS maps) that winds up through pines and rhododendrons over NT land to Aldworth House drive, near its junction with the access road to Foxholes.

Aldworth House, hidden in the trees on the left, was built in 1869 by the Poet Laureate, Lord Tennyson. Cross the drive and turn right along the bridlepath, parallel to the drive, to rejoin Tennyson's Lane near the entrance to the Blackdown lower car park.

△ *The Weald spreads out below the Hunter Memorial Seat*

Follow the sunken path to the right of the car park entrance, passing on the right the upper car park where there is a map of the area. At 917f, Blackdown is the highest point in West Sussex and has magnificent views from many points. It is largely covered with self-sown Scots pines, birches and rhododendrons with beeches on the lower slopes. Three species of heather, gorse and bracken fill the open spaces and bilberries fringe the paths.

Continue on the wide track southwards in the reverse direction of the Blackdown nature trail (indicated by grey concrete posts). At point 6, near a group of trees known as the Temple of the Winds, a small path on the left leads to the Hunter Memorial Seat and a direction finder. There are magnificent views to the greensand ridge at Leith Hill, the Weald, the Forest Ridges and a great length of the South Downs, at their nearest point barely 8m away.

Retrace your steps to the wide track and follow it for over ½m as it contours west and north, ignoring a bridlepath to the left and all crossing tracks as you pass several seats and viewpoints. At a junction of five tracks, take the second bridletrack on the left, first rising then dropping, then going straight over the next crossing track. At a T-junction, turn sharply left to head due south and then west. Pass to the right of the pond at Valewood Lodge to reach Fernden Lane. Turn right along the road briefly, then at Wadesmarsh Farm take the path on the right across fields and down the valley past the attractive seventeenth-century Valewood Farmhouse. In June the hillside to the right is brightly coloured with rhododendrons.

Cross a string of millponds into Lowder Mill Road. Turn right by Stedlands Farm, then left on the higher of two paths that leads steeply up Stedlands Hill as a sunken lane. You pass over two minor roads and down to the Petworth Road in Haslemere.

Turn left, with Collards House opposite – the point where the short-cut rejoins the main route. Walk along the road then go right into the pretty and wide High Street. Both roads contain interesting listed buildings from the fifteenth to the nineteenth century, often behind later frontages. There are two old inns and Haslemere Educational Museum (sixteenth-century in part) on the eastern side of the High Street; on the western side, past the Georgian Hotel and next to Tudor Cottage (sixteenth-century), a plaque signifies the start of the Greensand Way long-distance footpath.

Turn left on to the path between houses to reach Church Lane, then left again over the railway and, keeping the church on your left, go up High Lane. Take the enclosed path on the left up to Weydown Road and down to Bunch Lane. Turn left briefly, cross a stream and follow the lane on the right past Little Stoatley Farmhouse, steeply up Stoatley Hollow to Farnham Lane.

Turn right up the road and, just after a pillar box and opposite a house named Little Scotstoun, take a signposted path on the left. Follow this, ignoring all crossing tracks and horse tracks, as it winds first through woodland and then over more open heathland over Hindhead Common. The final stretch climbs to the A3 road at Hindhead, opposite the starting point.

△ *Wild rhododendrons grow in several areas on the walk*

125

Useful information

The NT owns and protects well over 500,000a in England, Wales and Northern Ireland – about one per cent of the total land area. It is perhaps best known for its great country houses with their gardens and parks, but it was not for these that the organization came into existence in 1895. At that time the countryside itself and its smaller buildings were under threat, as towns and suburbs spread and places like the Lake District began to feel the full impact of the newly-mobile population. The first property acquired by the NT was a mere $4\frac{1}{2}$a of clifftop at Dinas Oleu, near Barmouth in Gwynedd. Its first building was the historic but modest mid fourteenth-century Clergy House at Alfriston, East Sussex.

Today, the NT looks after 450m of the finest unspoilt coastline. It has 1,100 tenanted farms, and cares for one-quarter of the Lake District National Park and one-tenth of Snowdonia. There are huge tracts of NT land in the Peak District, South Wales, Dorset and Somerset, together with parts of the Malvern and Shropshire Hills and the Isle of Wight, and there are innumerable other NT properties scattered across the country.

When you are walking on NT land, look searchingly at your surroundings. Note how the woods, fields and copses are managed, how the paths are laid out and maintained, and how local features such as stiles, walls, barns and fences are looked after and renovated in keeping with the character of the countryside.

The NT's twin aims of access and conservation take time and money. The work is based on detailed management plans, often drawn up in consultation with bodies such as the Nature Conservancy Council, Countryside Commission, local county councils, and naturalists' and archaeological trusts. Walkers who gain pleasure from NT facilities can reciprocate by joining the NT – a charity that looks after large tracts of land and buildings for you, and for future generations, to enjoy for ever.

The National Trust, Central Office, 36 Queen Anne's Gate, London SW1H 9AS; phone 01-222 9251

Membership enquiries to: The National Trust, Membership Department, PO Box 30, Beckenham, Kent BR3 4TL; phone 01-650 7263

The National Trust, **East Anglia Regional Office**, Blickling, Norwich NR11 6NF; phone Aylsham (0263) 733471

The National Trust, **Thames & Chilterns Regional Office**, Hughenden Manor, High Wycombe, Bucks HP14 4LA; phone High Wycombe (0494) 28051

The National Trust, **Southern Regional Office**, Polesden Lacey, Dorking, Surrey RH5 6BD; phone Bookham (0372) 53401

The National Trust, **Kent & East Sussex Regional Office**, The Estate Office, Scotney Castle, Lamberhurst, Kent TN3 8JN; phone Lamberhurst (0892) 890651

London Natural History Society, c/o British Museum (Natural History), Cromwell Road, London SW7 5BD

Sussex Trust for Nature Conservation, Woods Hill, Shoreham Road, Henfield, West Sussex

Essex Naturalists' Trust, Fingringhoe Wick Nature Reserve, South Green Road, Fingringhoe, Colchester, Essex CO5 7DN

Surrey Trust For Nature Conservation, Hatchlands, East Clandon, Surrey GU4 7RT

Ramblers' Association, 1/5 Wandsworth Road, London SW8 2LJ; phone 01-582 6878

Ordnance Survey, Romsey Road, Maybush, Southampton SO9 4DH

Walkers are advised to plan their outings using current NT information for details of opening days and times and admission fees. Two invaluable sources are *Properties of the National Trust* and the *Properties Open* booklets relating to the region in question.

Acknowledgements

Thanks are due to the following people for devising routes and writing walk accounts and features:
David Black, Millie and Ray East, Janet Goodwin, Arthur Hollock, John Malley, Dorothy Nail, Peter Nevell, Jane Parker, Enid and Jeanne Perryman, Roy Plascott, Barbara and Kenneth Pring, Geoffrey Pyman, Robert Tanner, Stanley Thorley, Robin Wright, Anne Yarrow

Thanks also to the following for their help:
John Fielding, Christopher Hanson-Smith, Pam Horner, Jim Monahan, Norman Price, Stephen Povey, Jim Spencer and the Mole Valley Ramblers, Ramblers' Association, Ian Swinney, Barry Thornber, John Wilson

Illustrations by Andrew Aloof, Rosalind Hewitt, Christine Hart-Davies ARMS, SGA, Aziz Kahn

Walk and locator map   Cooper West

Art work visualiser   Mike Trier

Additional photography   John Bethell – page 51 – courtesy of The National Trust.

The publishers are grateful to the following companies and individuals:
Blacks of Holborn for camping equipment, Nikon UK Ltd for camera equipment, Fred and Kathy Gill, Format Publishing Service, Diana Greenman and Jane Parker